# Everyone Has a Story to Tell:

## *Forty Years of AFS*

# Everyone Has a Story to Tell:

## *Forty Years of AFS*

By M. E. Eiseman

The **M** Press
Milwaukee, Wisconsin

# Acknowledgments

Everyone who has had a story to tell about AFS over the past 40 years has had a role to play in the inspiration for this book. A few individuals have been especially important in its creation and I would like to thank them for their support, interest and their "AFS Spirit."

To my folks, Barb and Bob Eiseman, I hope you're glad I got you into AFS 15 years ago!

To my husband and editor, Andrew Muchin: I'm glad we're still friends! I couldn't have done this without you.

To those staff members of AFS who went out of their way to help, in alphabetical order:

Robert "Apple" Applewhite, Margaret Connolly, Susan Ford, Deb Frueh, Donna Gorski, Linda Hall (and the whole Development Department), Edie Holbrook, Bill Orrick, Rosemary Price, Scott Ramey, Jan Shannon, Murray Shaw, Ann Souronis, Dana Strauss, Doris Wilkins, Jean Wine, Cynthia Wornham and Rob Zopf.

A special thank you to Bill Orrick, director of AFS Archives, who generously donated time, patience and his unpublished history of the first 30 years of AFS and to Cynthia Wornham for the many hours spent as liaison.

Cover photos of front porch scenes around the world are courtesy of the Greater Kansas City Area AFS returnees. Cover design is by Scott Design, Brooklyn, New York.

To my friends on the Milwaukee Area AFS Rep Council and AFS volunteers the world over: THANKS FOR EVERYTHING!

Everyone Has a Story to Tell: Forty Years of AFS

Copyright © 1987 by M. E. Eiseman, The M Press  Milwaukee, Wisconsin
Library of Congress Catalog Number 87-090512
ISBN 0-9618597-0-9
Photos and articles reprinted with permission from AFS International/Intercultural Programs, Inc.

# Preface

It's an act of faith in something to open your home to an adolescent (or adult) from another culture, but it is a risk that thousands of families take each year. In the process, you may get to know your own family better and learn to love someone whose skin is a different color or who comes from halfway around the world.

Forty years ago, the founders of AFS International Scholarships -- the volunteer ambulance drivers of the American Field Service -- were sure that bringing young people from war-torn Europe to spend one year in the United States would be universally meaningful, even though the experience itself was personal.

Alongside the French in WWI and the British in WWII, the AFS volunteers developed friendships that personalized the wars. Their memories of people and families were more important than governments and ideologies, and this is what they sought to promote in their peace-time activities. Now, 40 years later, almost 158,000 people from 90 countries have been AFSers, having an affect on families all around the globe.

AFS has weathered many storms during its evolution, shaped by forces within and outside of its control. AFS International today is a far cry from the six-person, one-room office that served as headquarters in the early years, but, as you will see in this book, the focus has remained startlingly clear: **People can learn to understand and accept differences in other people and can even learn to love each other, too.** And if one person can achieve this rapport with one family, then there is increased hope for humanity. International, intercultural, interracial, interreligious, interurban -- name the gap and AFS has bridged it.

As I collected the stories that fill this book, I realized that each one illuminated a slightly different point of view or spoke with a different accent. Life-long volunteers or recent returnees, staff members or host siblings, stories and poems all make a contribution to the AFS whole and to this book.

I hope you can find your story somewhere in the following pages. But, if you read just one piece that makes you think, that challenges some prejudice, that startles you or strikes you as so funny that you have to retell it, then you, too, will have had an AFS experience. Welcome to the family!

*M E Eiseman*

*AFS Director General Stephen Galatti and Sachiye Mizuki on arrival in Chile.*

*Most people view AFS as an opportunity for personal or family development. But without the vision and dedication of the staff members, especially the Presidents, there could be no coordination, no direction, and AFS would be just a nice idea instead of a worldwide force for intercultural understanding and peace.*

# The Galatti Years: AFS Is

*Top: Stephen Galatti doing one of his favorite things -- meeting with AFSers. Bottom: Galatti and Caecilia in 1963. She wrote on the back of the original photo, "May I always be with you spiritually just like this picture. Oh, our dear daddy, you are so wonderful and I am so lucky that you like me...."*

To many people, Stephen Galatti *was* the American Field Service. From 1936, when he took over from A. Piatt "Doc" Andrew, he ran the field service from a crowded New York office, serving enthusiastically as Director General of the American Field Service until his death in 1964. By day he worked as a stockbroker, but he lived for AFS. His speech in September 1946, at the first reunion after the war for about 600 AFS ambulance drivers and their distinguished guests, British and French government officials, fueled the peacetime transformation of the AFS. This is how he put it:

"In the two wars they [the AFS men] carried over one million-and-a- half of your soldiers. They did this as volunteers, not one of whom went unthinkingly or unwillingly. Some were killed, some were wounded, and some made prisoner. What these men want me to tell you tonight is not what they did, but that, in doing it, they experienced the opportunity to mingle with you, to know you, and to realize that the men of your nations are their friends -- whether privates or generals or sergeants -- all the same kind of people, brothers under the skin, just as these AFSers represent the South, West, Midwest, the East -- all corners of the United States ... We send you this message: We were at your side during war because we believed in you; we will remain at your side during peace because we know that it can endure only if all of us can understand each other as we understand you."

Of course, the very next day, approximately 250 AFS members voted to make their organization permanent, establish a clubhouse and start an exchange of scholarships with foreign countries, in part reviving the French Fellowships (scholarships for university students) which had occupied them between the two world wars and adding the new dimension of high school-age students attending American preparatory schools.

The core of Galatti's team by the early 1950s included Sachiye Mizuki, George Edgell and Dorothy "Dot" Field. The basic elements of the program were set. Edgell was in charge of selection and placement of students coming to the U.S. He and Galatti sent out the Eagle Letters, full of advice and encouragement that came with the all-important monthly allowance. Sachi was in charge of Summer Program selection, arranging the bus trips and bringing out Our Little World (the returnees' newsletter whose editorship changed country each year). Dot had worked in the AFS office during wartime producing AFS Letters, a compilation of volunteers' letters which told of life in the service. Naturally, she was in charge of hospitality, correspondence and student welfare.

Galatti enlisted the former U.S. Ambassador

1

to Rumania, Robert Thayer Jr., and others to help expand the scope of AFS in the world. Every trip to an AFS gathering became an opportunity to establish the program in another city or country. AFS often relied upon the U.S. Embassy Cultural Affairs Officers or Fullbright fellows to help interview candidates, and when the Americans Abroad program got started, to help interview host families.

Galatti had the idea that anyone he met would be interested in the AFS. He would ask anyone for anything and wrote thousands of personal notes. He also believed that he should be involved in every detail of the operation. For example, there's a story about a girl whose host mother kept reading her mail. Dot Field showed him the girl's letter and he wrote back one of his famous notes:
"Dear So-and-So,
    If your mother reads your letters, she shouldn't."

He would have qualified for "frequent flier" bonuses as he traveled the world over, meeting with returnees and national committees overseas, and volunteers and students across America.

By the time of his death, AFS was established in 59 countries and handling more than 3,000 students per year.

*Top: Newsman Walter Cronkite with Stephen Galatti and students. Bottom: Galatti typically drawing a crowd in Torino, Italy*

*Even at the White House, Galatti was the AFSers' President.*

# The First Year, the First Bus Trip

The 28 students from seven European countries who had spent their year in East Coast prep schools had not seen much of America. Their contact with American families had been limited to school vacations. Galatti and the staff felt that the direct contact between individuals that had made the war-time experience so enriching was going to make AFS an exchange of personalities, not dossiers and money.

Carl Zeigler, a public relations man and former AFS driver from Chicago, and his wife Elinor persuaded Greyhound Bus Lines to donate a bus and driver for a 6,000-mile, 24-day tour. The Zeiglers, Dot Field and a young relative of Galatti chaperoned the trip from New York to the Rockies, south through Texas to New Orleans and then back through Washington, D.C., to New York. They went to 22 states in all, stopping along the way in home communities of AFS drivers or friends of Galatti's. No-one learned more than the driver, Bernard Foley, who wrote about his experiences for the October 1948 issue of The American Magazine:

"I thought I knew all about America. This trip made me feel like a dope. It was like exploring a new country. Some of the kids' comments made me squirm ... but more often made me swell with pride ...

"They drove tractors, watched steel being made, saw Indian dances, visited the White House ... The reception the kids got when they came out into the broad, open spaces of interior America made a deeper impression on them than any other single thing in the 'total picture' of America.

*Dwight D. Eisenhower addressed AFS students during two presidencies. He was official starter of the first AFS bus trip in 1948, when he was President of Columbia University. He continued his informal talks from 1952-59, as U.S. Chief Executive. Ike's speeches to the students were thoughtful and encouraging, as you will see from some of his comments of July 12, 1955:*

*"Never forget, you have got a long time to live in this world, and so you want to make certain that you do your part with a full comprehension of the facts and with an open-minded, conciliatory attitude toward the other fellow's viewpoint. But, never sacrifice the basic principle that the human being is the important thing on this planet.*

*"I am not sure, youngsters, why I got so serious just as I came out here to see you all, but possibly it is because I have spent so much of my life with young people -- young soldiers -- young people. I like them, and trust them. And honestly, my confidence in what you -- this group, those like you, those that come after you -- can do in this world is unbounded.*

*"Don't ever let anyone tell you you are licked."*

"In the East, they had gotten a cordial but prim, polite welcome. As they entered the Midwest, they were, to be frank, nervous. They had read in Eastern newspapers a lot about the Midwest's alleged isolationism and suspicion of 'furriners' ... People in Omaha, Des Moines, and North Platte ... seemed tickled to see them. What

startled the Europeans almost as much as the generosity was the easy-going informality and lack of 'airs' of our people in authority. Cops always stopped to banter with the kids. The Mayor of New Carlisle, Indiana, horsed around with them and gave them a big wooden key to the town.

## Town Reaps Picnic Harvest

When they were planning the itinerary of the first bus trip, I suggested that they go to my hometown of New Carlisle, Indiana, and I'd ask my mother and her friends, who had been good volunteers for the Field Service during the war, if they would put on a "real old-fashioned pot-luck country picnic" for the kids, and everybody's invited.

I had gone out there during the war to raise money from the mothers and I had gone to them again and given a speech to raise money for the scholarships. I knew my mother could run that picnic with help from everybody else. She almost died, but they did it; there must have been 200 or 300 people there, all over the farm, on the lawns and so on. And the young people had a marvelous time. They slept in houses all around the village.

This changed the outlook of the whole town, 'cause they'd been very isolationist, very anti-European, very nervous about foreigners, and this opened it up. It's a key story of what we were trying to achieve: to build as broad an experience as possible.

**Bill Hooten**, WWII driver and AFS staff member, 1946-49

*Shipboard travel is now a thing of the past but many AFSers have fond memories of their ocean crossing. Top: Returnees joined Robert Applewhite on the S.S. Seven Seas in June 1966 to provide orientations for European-bound Americans Abroad students. Center and below: Aboard the S.S. Ryndam, AFSers at play.*

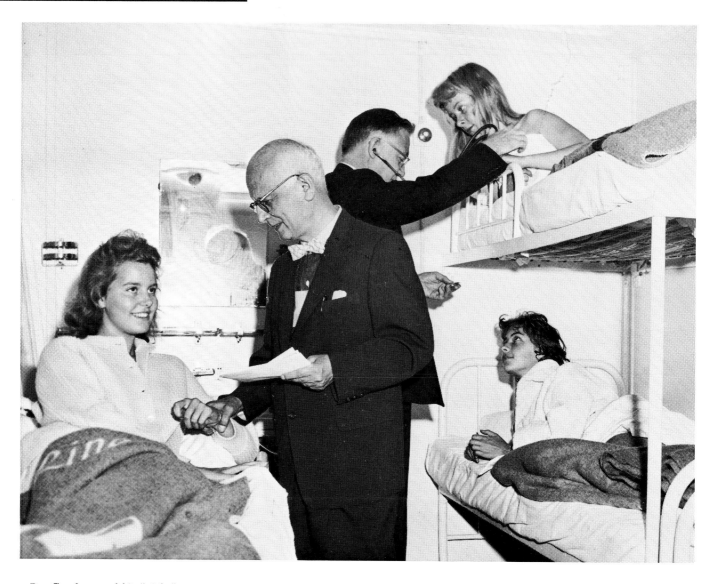

*Dr. Gardner and his "girls."*

# Assorted Aches and Pains: Dot and the Doctors

From the beginning, AFS has been fortunate to have first Dr. William A. Gardner and then returnee Dr. Bill Brown on staff to review the medical part of all applications and to consult on problems that arise during the program year. With thousands of students on the program throughout the world, an assortment of aches and pains is to be expected.

In the early years, Dot Field would write medical situation reports which Stephen Galatti personally reviewed, often writing little notes to the students. Since these reports were internal memos, they are decorated with his sketches of the accidents.

Let's look at some of the reported injuries from 1964:

In May, a boy in Shamrock, Texas, shot his left foot with a 22-calibre rifle. It was a clean wound, but what was he doing with the rifle? A French girl fell off her bicycle and was taken to the hospital for x-rays. Baseball never seemed especially dangerous, but a Brazilian boy was hit by a baseball which broke his nose and a French student playing the game needed five stitches in his head after running into another boy.

There were numerous cases of

German Measles and strep throat, one possible appendicitis and one emergency appendectomy, and lots of students reported feeling run down. To the Turkish girl who had a throat bug, Galatti suggested that she shouldn't keep her mouth open.

One boy who had previously grazed his face on the school diving board was again in the report after diving into too-shallow water: He hurt his teeth and nose quite badly and Dot hoped the school had good insurance!

Injured in the line of duty was a Thai girl who lost her voice on an AFS speaking tour, and Dot Field, who got a splinter in her finger while cleaning up before receiving Area Representatives for cocktails (with a typical Galatti note about not drinking cocktails)!

Early June brought on a rash of ankle injuries, a "nasal hemorrhage" -- which Galatti thought could have been called a "bloody nose" -- a soccer-induced dislocated shoulder and various other ailments.

An Argentine boy was in a car accident (he was driving!), and another boy ran into a door and broke his toe. There were two accidents involving horses and three others involving cars.

And, this may be the most unusual one of all: While on a camping trip in Arizona, a German girl reported that a tree fell on her tent because of high winds. A plate cut her hand and her leg was bruised, BUT the family dog was "done killed daid." Responded Galatti, "Poor Doggie."

**M.E.**

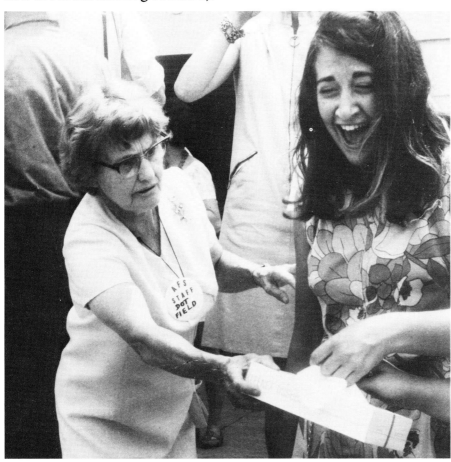

*Dot Field in action.*

## The First Midway: They Could Hardly Sleep

In 1954, we decided to organize a "Midway," a pre-departure gathering for all the students. I was on the Board of Education in Dobbs Ferry, New York, so naturally, Steve [Galatti] thought I would have some pull. I arranged to get the high school for five days in August, and I borrowed a lot of school busses from other schools that had AFSers in them to help us with various local trips for the kids.

I got the Rotary Club to give a big barbecue one night to feed them all and the Lions' Club fed them another night. I got Hugh Leighton, who owned and ran Leighton's Restaurant, to cater breakfasts and lunches at the school cafeteria for some very nominal fee.

We got 425 folding cots from Civil Defense through the Red Cross. We rented sheets (no blankets since it was August), and we lined the cots up in two gymnasiums, one for the girls and one for the boys. And the most dramatic and outstanding memory we all have of the whole gathering was that the cots were just useless -- left over from '39 or '40.

At least 35 or 50 of them would collapse each night and drop to the floor with this terrible noise in these huge gyms, and the students would be slammed to the floor while they were asleep, waking everybody up about hourly, and really banging up some of the kids.

It sounds hilarious, but I don't really think it was. And The Boss [Galatti] always said it was a huge success, translated to mean that I had managed to get almost everything free.

**Elaine Koehl**, unpaid staffer, Board member Arkie's mom

# First-Class Accommodations

Two things stand out in my memory from my AFS experience in the summer of '56: the beginning and the end. I arrived in Barcelona and met the members of family and the servants (who outnumbered family!). The first morning, I got up, made my bed and went downstairs for breakfast. When I got back to my room, the maid was there and she chewed me out: "If you do this, I won't have a job. Please don't make your bed anymore."

Two years later, my family hosted B. Nigel Gilson, who was the first student to come to the U.S. from South Africa. When I think of what he encountered when he came to live in Whitefish Bay, Wisconsin, I laugh at the comparison. He had never made his bed before and of course was expected to in our house. I definitely had the easier time adjusting.

The other strong memory is about my departure. The family was staying at Cadaces, on the Costa Brava, on their private island, so I had to go into town to catch the bus back to Barcelona.

My Spanish brother accompanied me to town, but we fooled around so long that when I got to the bus, all the seats were taken. I was told to climb on top.

I braced myself in a corner of the luggage rack and with a couple of Spanish companions and lots of luggage, rocked and rolled as the bus crossed the Pyrenees Mountains. I passed the time by singing, in Spanish, at the top of my voice, every song I knew. It was a class act.

**Colonel Thomas R. Stone,**
Director, Strategic Studies Institute, U.S. Army War College

# Harvard Bends the Rules

In the late 1950s and early '60s, Harvard University maintained very strict entry quotas. Usually, this meant limiting the number of students from any one high school to the valedictorian.

When a junior class valedictorian chose to go on AFS for her senior year, Harvard accepted the next best applicant from that graduating class. But trouble arose when the junior valedictorian's application arrived from Sweden and the admissions people wanted to offer her a place in the freshman class.

Harvard isn't in the Ivy League for nothing. Officials decided to accept this American girl as a Swedish student because she never graduated from her own high school!

*A typical Midway scene--1961, Washington, DC*

# Homecoming for $20 Worth of Worms

In the early 1960s, the monthly allowance for AFS students was $12. This was supposed to cover postage, personal supplies, an occasional movie and ice cream, but didn't really go very far. By November, it turned out that Mario had spent more than he had and had asked to borrow from his host brother, Stan. When I found out, I told him that wouldn't do and if he wanted to take a date to the Homecoming, he'd have to earn the money.

"But, AFS students can't work. How will I earn $20 to take a girl to the dance and buy her a flower and ...?" he asked. Obviously he didn't know me, yet! Almost anything can be turned into money, and so I took him out into the countryside and we set to work picking the stems of goldenrod where the gall wasps lay their eggs.

If you've ever seen the larvae, they look like bulbs grown into the stem. The fishermen use the worms for bait. I know this

because I'm a fisherman, and so Mario and I picked almost a thousand gall wasps and sold them to the fishermen for two cents each. He earned his $20 . Believe me, he earned it.

**Harry W. Rubinstein,**
Milwaukee, Wisconsin, host parent to Mario Perez, Argentina '61-62

*When in North Africa...*

# When in Indiana, Do as the Hoosiers Do

I think that the impact of placing Asian students in this country was really colossal -- I don't think anybody realizes how enormous that was.

For instance, in Valparaiso, Indiana, there was a boy from Borneo whose mother cooked outdoors. He happened to be placed with a very good family with four or five children (we found out that the Indonesian kids did better in big families). He went to church on Sunday and sang in the choir.

And then his father called me up in Milwaukee because I had visited there and was a little concerned about how primitive the boy was. The father said: "We're having a terrible time, because he won't bathe in the bathtub. He insists on bathing on the bathroom floor and the water leaks through to our kitchen." I went to see them and he was indeed bathing on the floor.

So I said to him, "You know, I've been in Jakarta, and I always remember they brought out those beautiful platters of vegetables that looked so beautiful, they were cooked just right."

And his face lifted up and I said: "Then, they did something that made me very unhappy. They threw peanut oil all over it."

And he said, "Don't you like oil?"

And I said, "No."

He said, "What did you do?"

I said: "I ate it. I was in your country. And, unless I'm sick, I eat it. Now, when you're in this country, you bathe in a bathtub. You're not in Borneo. You bathe in the tub, not on the floor. You're ruining the ceiling. You owe it to these people."

"Well, all right," he said, "but I won't use a washcloth."

**Jerry Madison**, early volunteer in Milwaukee, Wisconsin, former staff member (see story p.10 )

## Everyone Knows Mrs. Madison

*Jerry Madison, an AFS volunteer from Milwaukee, Wisconsin, left for a three-month trip to the South Pacific and Africa in late 1962. She developed AFS at every stop, meeting with the Ministers of Education, principals, teachers, returnees, host parents and U.S. Embassy personnel to try to establish coordinated, logical selection of AFSers and local host families. The following story is pieced together from an interview with AFS archives director Bill Orrick (done just before Madison's death in 1976) and the actual trip reports from the AFS Archives, which read like letters home:*

I was escorting a group of 37 American students across the Pacific and we stopped in Hawaii en route to Fiji, New Zealand and Australia. As we left Hawaii, I witnessed the most marvelous scene.

You know how the Hawaiians always send dancers to welcome and send off the cruise ships. Well, the AFS kids were sitting on the top deck in the moonlight singing back and forth to the Hawaiians on the dock. A beautiful moonlit night and the soft air and the music created such a lovely spirit that I always wished I could share it with others.

In New Zealand, we got a royal welcome by a mayor, and a big party. I had known a boy in the States whose father was a tribal head of the Maori, so they took me out there to a festival. He was a really nice kid and I had taken him to speak to a women's club back home.

He looked so very Polynesian in his grass skirt and he told them, "If I were wearing this at home, I wouldn't wear my shorts under it." You should have seen the expressions on the women's faces! They almost died.

From the South Pacific, we flew 24 hours in a prop plane (we refueled in Ceylon and stopped in the Mauritius, which are fascinating because they have this volcanic sand that's all black). We finally came to South Africa, where I made stops in Capetown, Durbin, Johannesburg, La Fontaine, and Port Elizabeth.

In Johannesburg, Clive Menell and his wife entertained me and I was escorted around by Deral Ross, a very capable returnee who would play a large role in developing AFS committees in many cities. Anyway, Clive was the person who took over the fledgling AFS

money on bars, and how you should save your money and take it home. And then they got up and marched out, and this was also something to see because they all went out in their own dance forms, in their different costumes.

In Johannesburg, the Menells had rented a building for the colored, the blacks, the Africans (I never know what to call them) to use for a music school because they were all so crazy about music. One Sunday afternoon, I went to this school and Clive and I were the only whites in the place, and they were all playing this jazz music which was terribly exciting. Outside the window they were doing a war dance, which was also exciting in a different way.

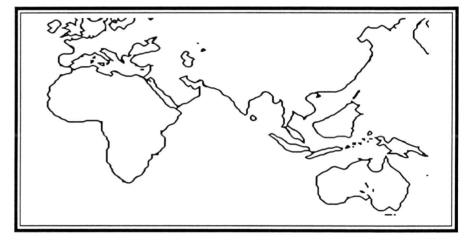

in South Africa when the founder, Mick Pennington, passed away.

The Menells were such fascinating people. They took me to one of their mines and I saw how they used an invented language to bridge the communication problems between the workers of different tribes. I was impressed but at the same time it was embarrassing to see these workers show off. We sat in a sort of tribal hut and all these people were in different costumes -- it was very colorful. And they sang their teaching songs about how you shouldn't spend your

Then I left for Swaziland and Rhodesia, and I began to notice the difference in how I was treated now that President Kennedy was in. The newspaper in Salisbury ran a front page story about me -- Granny Carries Message of Peace Around the World -- with a photo that makes me look like I had been decapitated! But I began to be invited places where before I had been standing at the door, saying, "Will you let me in?" and I was shown around to schools and met Ian Smith, the Prime Minister. There was a 9:00 curfew at night and it felt more sinister there than in South Africa.

From Salisbury, Rhodesia, I flew to Kenya and was met in Nairobi by a young man named Peter who grew up in the Rift country in a place with no windows and where they played in the "streets" with giraffes! I had been living and breathing AFS every day and every night, so after a few days in Nairobi, I went to the Tree Tops, which is a sort of safari hotel, for a two-day rest.

On the drive up, my driver asked me if I would like to walk down to the river. As I walked, I saw an alligator-- or a crocodile -- on the bank, opening his mouth. I started up the hill, I really got so excited. You can't imagine! And, as I was going up the hill, I looked up and there was a snake hanging from a tree. Well, I thought, "This is it. I've had it with Africa, I'm going to leave immediately." I can't even stand a garter snake.

Of course I didn't leave and in fact, when I got to the Tree Tops, there was an American couple who kept asking me what I was doing there. People were very surprised to find an American woman travelling alone through Africa.

I finally told the husband I was working for the AFS. Would you believe it, he said his was the first host family for an AFS student in Hartford, Connecticut.

Well, that's how it went. I continued on my journey to Uganda, where I found a number of young people who had been involved with the Field Service or the Peace Corps. There were really ardent young people like the Ericksons (Mary had been an American Abroad from Portland, Oregon) and others teaching for no money at all. I was a friend of Sir Frederick Crawford, who had been the Governor of Uganda and

# Black Consciousness-Raising 101

Peter Mulira came from Uganda for the 1958-59 program year. He was one of the very first black African AFS students, certainly the first Ugandan. He arrived at the airport with two spears and a shield of his tribe to protect himself.

My job was to pick him up at the airport and stay with him until his family came. I brought him back to the AFS Headquarters in New York, and we went to my desk.

I was trying to talk slowly to him and explain about the family that was coming to get him, and he just didn't look at me. He couldn't take his eyes off the file clerk, a very capable young black woman named Fanny Woods, who was walking back and forth in front of him, going from one file drawer to another in the cabinets next to my desk.

Finally, he asked me, "What tribe does she belong to?"

And that so startled me then, but I thought about it many times, particularly now when we all read about Africans, and they don't think of themselves in terms of nations at all. They think of themselves in terms of tribes, even inside the nations that we've artificially set up -- the British,

French. Why, they're still battling it out between their tribes.

He couldn't understand, nor could she. She was absolutely flabbergasted to be asked a question like that. She said, "I'm an American."

And he said again, "No, I mean, what tribe do you come from?"

**Elaine Koehl**, former full-time volunteer

retired to live in Rhodesia, so I had a really marvelous entree to get in and see the schools.

The schools were fascinating. In one, a teacher took me to the laboratory and he said, "You see all the bottles? We had to drink all the beer and gin first."

We had had a boy from Uganda in Milwaukee whose father was a head of a tribe. The boy's family came to the airport to see me off, all 90 of them. I also went out to their village for a festival day and drank that terrible beer and they played music and danced for me.

But, really, the schools were so poor that when I went back to Milwaukee, I asked the schools there to collect books to send to Uganda (especially, the trial copies of text books, things that would be useful for an

educational project like this) and we had the Smithsonian Institution ship them for us.

But from Dar es Salaam, Tanzania, there's only a one-track train to Kampala and when the chief went to collect the books, they wanted $115 for shipping costs. People are marvelous -- those folks in Milwaukee collected the money, people giving whatever they could, and sent it to them. We really supplied that whole school with books for about two years.

# Fascinating Washing Machine

I met a family who lived in a little town outside of Omaha who had never in their lives been anyplace. Maybe just to Omaha. Very nice, very simple lower

11

middle-class people. And they had a girl, Helena, from Salonica the year before, and I asked them how did this work? Because I know Greek girls are not always so easy.

And the mother said, "Well, you know, Helena was so interested in our washing machine, our automobile, our radio (or television, I don't know which)." And then the woman looked at me and said, "We went to Salonica."

So I asked, "How was it?"

"Well, they were lovely people. But you know, we had to go downstairs to get the water to bring into the house."

Afterwards, I went with the kids in Greece on a bus to Salonica, and we stopped at a little village, and do you know where I slept? In a chicken coop. They had a bed and they had all the wire up, and I slept in there.

I made it a point to go to Helena's house and it was really quite primitive. So I think those people, who had never been anyplace, had traveled all the way to Salonica, and they were really, I think, taken aback. No wonder Helena was overcome by a washing machine.

Interview with AFS volunteer and staffer **Jerry Madison** by Bill Orrick, 1976

*Americans Katherine Lowry (left) and Joyce Bartschi join Yoshiko Sadatoshi (1955 returnee) in a Japanese dinner, summer 1957.*

*Art Howe (right) with California volunteers.*

# Art Howe: Putting AFS in Order

When Galatti died in July 1964, the AFS world mourned. Then it was up to the Board of Trustees to find a successor who could put the house in order. With almost 4,000 students a year participating in AFS programs, it was no longer possible to run a "one-man-show" as Galatti had done. Arthur Howe Jr., AFS driver (WWII) and board member, then Dean of Admissions at Yale University, was chosen to be President, and Galatti's title of Director-General was retired. Howe's charge was to create a structure that would allow the programs to grow and implement modern management techniques.

For the six months between Galatti's death and Howe's assumption of duties, the board turned to Ed Masback, a Founding Member, Director and Treasurer of the Board of Trustees, and then long-time staff member George Edgell to serve as Acting Director General. The student programs were continued thanks to the work of Edgell, Sachiye Mizuki, Alice Gerlach, Robert Applewhite (known as "Apple") and other experienced members of the staff.

Their immediate challenge was the 50th Anniversary Convention of the American Field Service, scheduled for August 1964. The five-day convention, held in New York at the same time as the World's Fair, attracted more than 5,000 AFS supporters, 1,500 of whom were from outside the United States.

The years of Howe's presidency, 1965-71, were some of the most troubled times in recent AFS history. Dress codes were challenged (until the late '60s, girls were not permitted to wear shorts on travel days during the bus trip); Apple, still active in AFS as the Corporate Secretary, remembers the first time a bearded student's application arrived -- the picture was shown all around the office and created

13

quite a stir.

Unrest and anger were building in the hearts of youth and AFS was constantly challenged to seek students from less-developed nations, accept students who weren't necessarily the top of their class and be active in the fight against social injustice. The returnees were coming of age and wanted more say in the direction of the organization (and in 1966 they began to have representation on the AFS Board of Trustees).

Coinciding with the tumultuous feeling was a distressing drop in the number of participants. Rising inflation in the United States made it difficult to find host families and times were tough for AFS.

Howe's own assessment of his presidency was that, over time, he improved the relationship of staff and field (volunteers) by setting up Regional Conferences, workshops and participatory case studies to train volunteers in counseling and problem-solving, and by bringing in volunteers to share their expertise with staff members.

The relationship between the staff in New York and the myriad overseas offices also needed attention. For too long the staff had made decisions and told the offices overseas to obey. In the early '60s, the European returnees perceived AFS as having a series of bilateral arrangements to the detriment of multi-national cooperation. The European AFS organizations began to hold annual conferences to share methods.

The transition strategy (started by Galatti) of turning over the national organizations to returnees continued. Regional offices in Europe, Latin America and Seattle, Washington, were established. Subsequent conferences included the National Representatives, Overseas

*Art Howe with AFS supporters and President Richard Nixon.*

Representatives and leaders of the Returnee Organizations as well as staff from New York.

In addition, just about every seven years, the returnees would decide that their own leadership was too old and insensitive to the needs of the newest returnees. These organizations were constantly in flux, as the young professionals eventually would turn to other interests and organizations. Howe used to say that AFS couldn't be a "cradle-to-grave" operation and it was all right to let the returnees move on; they would always be AFSers at heart and could be called upon

later if necessary.

One thing Howe didn't accomplish was changing the name of the organization from the American Field Service to the Associated Field Service(s).

In the AFS International Newsletter, Vol. 2, No. 3 1986, he proposed the change again in conjunction with forming an International Emergency Corps (AFSIEC), an international, paramilitary, volunteer trained corps of men and women on two or three-year tours of duty maintained at alert for quick movement into any major disaster area worldwide.

# Art Howe on 'Denationalization' of AFSers

I am proud of the job AFS does in getting people back into their own societies reasonably effectively. Changed? Yes, but not alienated permanently.

Everybody is dislocated a little bit when he comes home, our own Americans Abroad as much as any, but one of the glories of this program has been its success in helping people back into the mainstream of their own places.

Of course they are going to be mobile people -- they were that kind when they first applied for AFS. I mean, you've got to be something of an adventurer if you're living in an African village and you apply for AFS -- yes, initiative and guts are needed. So the kinds of people we've attracted are bound to be mobile people just by pre-selection.

But, on the whole, we've sent back into developing and developed countries alike a lot of people with some tremendously significant awarenesses, very little affected by American propagandizing.

These people understand America a whole lot better and are therefore far less liable to misjudge us as a country. Positively put, they understand what we've said and why we say it.

I don't believe we've bought a lot of friends for America through AFS. I think we've produced thousands of people who make better citizens of an inter-related world. And the world has got to live together ... I've never been concerned very much about this being a propaganda thing.

The only times I do become concerned is when we begin to tell students what to think. There is a rising interest in what I call the indoctrination of students. What they should hope to look for, and what kind of experience they should have ...

I always welcome some distinctive skill ... because it can become one of the quickest handholds for meeting people and getting into things in a new place ... So, I've always stressed this concept, over and beyond those many fundamental qualities we hope for in every AFS student: intelligence, vigor, curiosity, flexibility, integrity and sensitivity. But I never felt it appropriate to stress the idea that participants should dig into world issues while they were AFSers ...

Political consciousness will be for most a natural outgrowth of the kind of experience we provide. I don't think we can make people become better world citizens by directly trying to teach them. We put them in relationships where this is likely to occur.

# The Eagle Letters

*The Eagle Letters went to all the students with their monthly allowance. Usually there was some advice, and some encouragement to promote AFS by selling more Christmas cards or helping to screen local Americans Abroad candidates. Galatti wrote the letters originally and included an account of his travels on behalf of AFS.*

*Over the years, they started to include a history of the organization and some thoughtful essays by George Edgell, the staff member in charge of student selection. In February 1965, he wrote the following:*

**The Word is 'Culture'**

A couple of months ago, I wrote you about "What is Education?" I did this because it is a subject I know you often are asked about and have to think about. But there is another word which I think you just as often hear or think of which is almost equally misunderstood, and

*Staff members at the 1967 Manila Conference included George Edgell (rear, left), Sachi Mizuki (rear, middle) and Art Howe (rear, right).*

which has so many very different meanings to different people ...

The word is "culture."

So much of the time, when I say "culture" I must expect that whoever I am talking to will think that I mean reading "good" books and listening to classical music and knowing about classical painting, etc. So much and no more. But the full meaning is immensely greater than this.

Of all living creatures, man is the only one that is not born with all the talents and equipment that he will need to live. All others merely need to be fed and protected until they have grown up -- and then they can operate alone, on their own.

But if you merely fed and protected a child until he was 15 years old or so, and then turned him loose, naked, with no knowledge and no tools, he would quickly die.

You would have failed to provide him with that platform of culture without which none of us can exist.

One part of this culture is knowledge. But ask yourself how important, relative to each other, different items of knowledge are. I know that there is a celebrated statue of Buddha in Kamakura in Japan -- and have seen it and would recognize a picture of it.

Play me a few bars of Beethoven's Ninth Symphony and I can tell you what it is. This is the sort of thing so many people mean by "culture."

But many thousands of years ago, someone learned a fact that is now common knowledge to nearly everyone in the world -- that if you take the seed of a plant, bury it in the earth and give it water, another plant will grow up like the plant you took the seed from.

Compared to this piece of knowledge, my knowledge of the Buddha at Kamakura and

Beethoven's Ninth Symphony is like pebbles beside a big mountain.

And then there are *tools*. My hands and nails and teeth are hopelessly weak. I cannot exist for even one day without using a

*Ecuadoran Reynaldo Barcia (1982-83 to Powers, Michigan) teaching civilized eating.*

variety of tools to multiply my strength. And along with the tools goes *skill* -- I must understand how to use them and be practiced in using them.

All this knowledge and these tools and skills have been built up and added to by men throughout thousands of years. And the amount has now grown so great that no one man can possess more than a tiny fraction of the culture

that he needs inside himself. I have one small selection of it. But, in order to live, I need the help of hundreds of other people who have their own, different selections of it. I cannot make the suit that I am wearing. I cannot even weave the cloth or spin the thread it is made of. And this is only one small thing. In hundreds of other ways I must depend upon other people and their special cultures.

All this dependence that everybody has upon so many other people then leads to a fourth element in culture -- *attitudes*. We must all live together and interact with each other effectively. To do this, we must have certain rules. I must know what to expect from other people: what they will do and what they will not do. I must know what is "right" and "good" and "proper," and guide my own actions and judge the actions of others accordingly.

So what is "right?" Who is "cultured" or "uncultured?"

Doesn't it boil down to the fact that there are a lot of different, but each perfectly satisfactory, ways to live? I certainly grant that there are some basic moral principles and ways of behaving that are common -- or should be common! -- to all mankind. But the person who is so proud of his knowledge of classical occidental music becomes an ignoramus when you play some Chinese music to him. The Indian who customarily eats most dishes with his fingers eats in fully as graceful and sanitary a way as someone who eats with knife and fork -- or with chopsticks.

So, even with my Buddha at Kamakura and my Beethoven's Ninth Symphony, when someone says "culture" to me, I try to think of all the vastness that this word really includes and so keep my opinion of my own culture a humble one.

From The Eagle Letters

*One of the ways AFS raised money was through the sale of Christmas cards designed by participants in an annual competition for most sales and best design, announced in The Eagle Letters. Two winning designs were "AFS Flags" by Judith Leon, Americans Abroad to Brazil, 1967; and "Footsteps in the Snow" by D. Bruce Stone, Americans Abroad to Japan, 1955.*

## AFS Lasts a Lifetime

I think the fact that Tom Gabelin, our AFS son in 1961-62, came from Germany has made it easier to keep up the connection over the past 25 years. If he had come from Indonesia or Japan even, it would have been harder. I went back through my photo album and made a list of the years our families have connected.

His aunt and grandfather had moved to New York from Krefeld (near Dusseldorf) just after World War II and settled on Long Island. I wondered at placing Tom so close to family, but it worked out fine and he didn't visit them until Christmas time. She and I have since become very close friends. We got to meet Tom's father in the fall of 1962 and then Tom's mother came the following spring with her father.

We planned our first trip to Europe in 1963 and of course went to stay at Tom's family's apartment in Krefeld. Tom was born in Thereisenstadt concentration camp in Czechoslovakia, where his parents and maternal grandmother were sent two months before his birth. They were both "mischlinge" --- of mixed blood -- children of two mixed marriages and therefore barred from marrying a "full-blooded Aryan." Both grandmothers, not religious Jews, had married Socialists who were non-believing Catholics.

Thereisenstadt was a show and transfer camp, not a death camp, and there were plenty of doctors willing to assist at a birth. We felt a special connection to him since we are Jewish, and as we celebrated our holidays, we explained things to him throughout the year.

Speaking of explanations, I found the biggest difference between having an AFSer and your own children was that your own kids understand your attitudes

*Then and now: Thomas Gabelin and family in 1985 and with three fellow AFSers (from left): Kurt Rangstrup of Denmark, Kahalida Matin of Pakistan and Odile Burgoyne of France.*

without saying things and you have to explain every stance to your AFSer. But by the end of the year, he knew full well his American father's attitudes. I think that's how a family grows together.

Well, back to our family saga.

Tom went back to finish his schooling and then enrolled at the University of Bonn, where he met Klaudia. He was specializing in psychology, which he had been exposed to in a two-hour elective at

Newton South High School and that opened up a whole world to him. He married Klaudia and they had two children, Marianne and Eva-Marie, while still students.

We went in May 1969 to meet Klaudia and the girls. "You know, Mom, I was your first daughter-in-law," she said. I hadn't really thought of it. Then the visits became more frequent. They came to see us in 1972 and we all attended our youngest son Philip's wedding in Paris that year.

They visited us in Boston again in 1975, we went there in 1976, they came here in 1977, we went in 1978 and in 1981, Marianne and Eva-Marie (teenagers already) came and spent April vacation with us in Cambridge. They became close friends with our second-oldest granddaughter, Nancy, and invited her to go that summer for a five-week stay. Now we have the second-generation exchange"!

**Janet Kaplan**, host mother to **Thomas Gabelin**, Germany, 1961-62 at Newton South H.S., Newton, Massachusetts

# Kindness Repaid

In 1968, I was a full-time staff person for AFS and I went to help conduct a Saturday workshop in southern New Jersey. During a break, a woman approached me shyly and said that she thought someone at AFS should hear the following story:

Her chapter in New Jersey had seen a letter to the editor in the local paper addressed to the people in her town from an American woman. The woman and her husband had been vacationing in Istanbul when the husband died suddenly. News of his death was in the next edition of the Istanbul newspaper, including the hotel where the couple was staying.

Suddenly, the woman, grieving and totally alone in a foreign country, heard a knock on the hotel room door. Her visitor was a young man, an AFS returnee who had spent his year in that New Jersey town.

He told the unhappy woman that he had read of her misfortune in the paper and had come to help her in any way he could, as he had been helped so much by the townspeople in New Jersey. He wanted to repay all their kindness to him by helping an American in need. He then spent the next few days aiding the poor woman in all the arrangements which had to be made to transport the husband's body back to the U.S.

She was so overwhelmed by the kindness of a stranger that she felt compelled to share the story with the New Jersey town which had hosted the Turkish AFSer. In almost 20 years, I've never forgotten the story.

**Nancy Vidal Mahler** France-US 1958-59

*Nancy Vidal Mahler (see above), like many other staffers, started as a shipboard chaperone. Their work was coordinated by the AFS Travel Department, pictured at right, in 1957.*

## AFS Career Goes the Distance

When the superintendent of the Great Western Sugar Co. plant in Scotts Bluff, Nebraska, was transferred to Billings, Montana, about two weeks before school started in 1953, he put in a call to the superintendent of schools.

His family had agreed to host a Swedish girl and didn't want to leave her behind in Scotts Bluff. Would it be all right if she attended school in Billings? As the School Dean at the time, I said sure we were going to take in that student, and that's how Kerstin Menander became the first AFSer in Montana.

I had no official AFS title at the beginning. For just two high schools in Billings, I would answer questions and eventually help start chapters. When AFS came up with the idea of an Area Rep in the late '60s, I became one.

I never even thought about how big the area was; like Topsy, the doll from "Uncle Tom's Cabin," it just growed. Most of my AFS work was done by phone since I was working at school, so I didn't do much driving around the territory. I do remember taking students to new towns and asking to make a presentation to the local Rotary or women's club. I thought then, and still think now, that AFS is educationally sound and that's why I was promoting it. I guess I started every chapter in Montana east of the Rockies. Credit AFS-USA board member Floyd van Weelden for his work in Montana west of the Rockies.

In 1971, after we held some well-attended spring conferences, I got a wonderful idea to hold the statewide conference in fall at Big Sky, the ski resort started by Chet Huntley. Since he was a

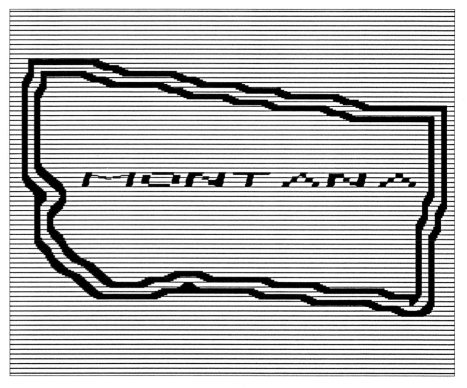

nationally known newsman with international experience, we thought he would be interested and give us a good deal. In fact, Mr. Huntley welcomed us personally the first two years and gave a most inspirational talk about the importance of global awareness.

In 1974, our Big Sky conference was cancelled due to the oil embargo. You see, the gas stations were closed on Sundays and people were driving hundred of miles each way to the conference and couldn't get home without stopping for gas! Montana is the fourth largest state, more than 600 miles from east to west and more than 400 miles from north to south. Even the people in Billings were 125 miles from Big Sky; it just wasn't feasible any longer.

The next year, the chapter in Lewistown (at the equi-center of the state) wanted to host the conference, and they did such a fine job that they have been host to all subsequent statewide

conferences.

I finally realized just how big the area was when one of the Chapter-Starting Reps, Judy Bailey from Oregon, asked to see my area. We got in the car and traveled 1,130 miles, and this was before the area got very big.

A chapter was organized in Watford City, North Dakota, and they wanted to join with Montana rather than North Dakota activities, which were mostly in the east. At the same time, chapters in Cody and Powell, Wyoming, wanted to join our area because they were only 35 miles from the Montana state line. When we got through, the area measured 1,630 miles around. If I didn't have someone from AFS with me to travel the circuit, my husband would go, but I didn't usually make the whole loop in one trip.

We developed self-reliant leadership in the chapters, and I intervened only if necessary. At a Rep Conference in Monterrey, California, I heard a Rep from

Los Angeles say, "I don't know what you expect me to do. It is 35 miles to my farthest chapter and I can't believe you want me to get in my car and travel all that way." I had a good laugh at that, because there wasn't a single chapter in my area *within* 35 miles.

Another part of my AFS career was more personal. At conferences we Reps used to bemoan the fact that we were born too soon and couldn't be participants. When AFS World described an opportunity for adults, particularly educators who were well-versed in AFS to be sent to talk about AFS and find out about how AFS was run in other countries, I applied and went to the United Kingdom with four other educators. We were together in London and then I boarded the train to Edinburgh, Scotland, and lived with a family on my own AFS experience.

My host mother, Doris McArthur, was a widow 15 years older than I, but her daughter, Jillian, had been an AFSer the same year my daughter, Susan (Gamill), went to Finland, so we had a common bond and had a marvelous time. Jillian subsequently moved to New Zealand after she married an Aussie and then her mother moved there, too. Years later, when my husband Lowell and I went to New Zealand to see Jillian and Doris, we rented a motor home to motor around New Zealand by ourselves, and I'm convinced it was my experience in Scotland that made us adventurous enough to do it.

Once Lowell and I had both retired, I realized that there were capable people to take over the area and I became a diagnostic counseling rep to ween myself: After 30 years, I couldn't give it up entirely. We ended up hosting a boy for six months last year, a part of the AFS experience we had been denied because of my administrative position. But, I have no regrets and lots of fond memories, and tell everyone that "AFS is an incurable disease and once you catch it, there's nothing you can do but enjoy it."

**Sue Hutton,** Area Rep and chapter starter for Montana for 30 years, mother of Susan (first year-program AA to Finland, 1958), grandmother of Laura Gamill (Montana-France, 1986-87), diagnostic counseling rep, AFS educator to Scotland, co-founder of the U S. Domestic Program

*AFS Chapters often commemorate their activities and students with a quilt. This 25th anniversary quilt was crafted by the Fergus Falls, Minnesota, Chapter in 1981.*

## Comic Genius an AFSer

Art, at its highest level, transcends words and cultural viewpoints. Whether in painting or performance, it is the goal of artists to communicate. Some artists, like Bill Irwin (US-Ireland, 1967-68) succeed.

Irwin was a 1984 recipient of the five-year MacArthur Foundation grant for his artistic achievement. If the MacArthur Foundation says he's a genius, believe it. Carefully researched, these grants are bestowed upon geniuses in a variety of fields and one does not apply for them.

Bill says he is an actor/writer. Other people know him only as Willy the Clown, or have seen him in his vaudvillesque one-man

shows and may think of him as a comedian or comedic performer. In all his roles, he is a thinking person to whom things happen. His clowning around has purpose and perspective.

Bill's family moved often when he was growing up. So, he learned adaptability, and by the time Bill was a senior in high school, he was ready to try a new place, moving because he wanted to.

As it turns out, Bill credits AFS for a big part of who he is. "It got me out of sheltered suburban American existence at an early age," he says.

AFS placed him in Belfast,

*As the AFS dress code was relaxed in the 1960s, AFSers found many ways to express themselves.*

Northern Ireland, and he lived with a very committed, activist family. Although "The Troubles," as they are called, did not surface until after Bill returned to the US, he was very aware of his family's politics. "Their strong commitment to an ecumenical problem-solving approach and their pride in living on an integrated (religiously) street impressed me," he explains.

Bill figures that "your adolescent years, well, you need to

have them be a little miserable. I'm glad my point of view got turned upside down." (By the way, this preceded his acrobatic comedy.)

The following story is a case in point:

"I was in the school play and I was so glad to become 'The Englishman' in Wuthering Heights instead of just 'the American kid,'" he recalls. "To be in the play, I didn't have to contend with a language barrier, or so they said, but I practiced a perfect BBC announcer's accent. The amazing thing is that after the performance, people came up to me and remarked on how I had 'lost my accent.'"

Ireland left its mark on him. He mentioned dreams, sometimes nightmares, about being there for the first 10 years after he returned to the US. "I haven't gone back partly because it would be too painful to see what I hear it's like. I've been awfully close, though, and I may yet return," he admits.

Bill's career as the premier clown has led him to tour France and Italy. He has lived in Malta and participated in a cultural delegation to Vietnam. He lives in Greenwich Village in New York City but has spent the last two summers doing theater in La Jolla, California.

Now freed from the necessity of earning a living by his grant money, Bill is traveling even more, performing benefits and shows. "I think that having AFS as a formative experience, along with the moving around that our family did, has prepared me to accept the enormous amount of travelling that I now do," he says. "It can be really tough." It can be really rewarding, too.

**M. E.**

*Naomi Ishahara of Japan became a star during 1981 when AFS filmed her year in Goshen, Connecticut, for the documentary "A World of Difference."*

## Neither Rain, Nor Sleet, Nor Civil War ...

Unfortunately, the governments of many countries in the family of AFS nations are unfriendly to one another. Cyprus is a nation unfriendly to itself. It is divided into Greek and Turkish sections, separated by a "Green Line" United Nations-patrolled zone. Amazingly, twice AFS Cyprus has managed to rise above the political situation on the island and function in spite of the problems.

In 1963, AFS President Stephen Galatti and Vice-President Robert Thayer made a special trip to meet with the Greek Cypriot Minister of Education and with the Turkish education authorities about establishing an AFS program there. The groundwork had been done by the US Embassy and USIS (United States Information Service) staff in the Cypriot capital, Nicosia, who assured Galatti of cooperation and support.

Since USIS was the most appropriate body to handle the operation, Cultural Affairs Officer Kristine Konold, helped by Frixos Yerolemou and Doghan Mehmet, Greek and Turkish Cultural Assistants, respectively, took over selecting the first group of Cypriot AFSers. It was hard going at first. USIS was unfamiliar with AFS paperwork and requirements and often had to improvise.

Moreover, there was pronounced reluctance from parents to allow their children to travel so far away from home, especially for the girls. Cyprus society in the '60s was still tied to tradition, and a teenager's trip to the US for an entire year seemed frightening. However, at the end of the first application period, we

were delighted to observe that the response was sufficient to provide for a selection of eight Cypriot AFSers, including two Turkish Cypriot girls.

A more serious and continuing difficulty has been the political instability aggravated by the Greek-Turkish bi-communal character of Cyprus. The new Cypriot state was only three years old in 1963 and ethnic politics and sensitivities played an important role everywhere. We had to steer carefully through conflicting interests to avoid antagonizing one side or another. As the program progressed, we established a rough ratio (to host or send) for each community and separate selection procedures. This, as expected, occasionally produced some confusion and duplication of effort.

It is a tribute to the ideals and methods of AFS that its record since 1963, when intercommunal strife divided the population, has provided one of the few instances of real cooperation between the two communities. The program's two main functionaries, Frixos on the Greek side and Doghan on the Turkish, have never failed to work hand-in-hand and secured regular participation throughout this period. This has not been easy to achieve and reflects the determination and dedication on the part of both men.

Between 1963 and 1976 the program expanded considerably on both sides. Initial feelings of hesitation and doubt gave way to enthusiasm and confidence. Applications began to be received from all parts of the island and all levels of society. In a short time, girls showed as much interest as boys and competition for places became intense.

No history of this period in Cyprus could be complete, however, without special reference to the hostilities of July

1974. The fighting occured only two weeks after the arrival in Cyprus of six American girls for the summer AFS program, and they underwent the terrors of war in company with the Cypriot population.

Two of them were living in houses that were almost on the confrontation line in Nicosia. Two others, in Famagusta, left their new homes for a safer place only minutes before their houses were hit by air bombardment. In the midst of shelling, bombing and gunfire, USIS Director David Grimland and Frixos managed to move them into the American Embassy and onward to Britain's military base in Cyprus, from which they were evacuated.

Meanwhile, 13 Cypriot students, undergoing the same dangers, almost despaired of their chances for travelling to the US for the regular one-year program. Transportation facilities were in chaos, with the island not only divided but sealed off from the rest of the world. The American Embassy decided to act on a report that a Greek ship would try to sail into Limassol, the harbor city in the south.

The Cyprus Broadcasting Corporation was persuaded to carry announcements that the Greek Cypriot AFS students should head for Limsassol and try to board the vessel. Frixos installed himself at the port, and when the S.S. Patra arrived he arranged for the passage of the nine. Miraculously, all nine got the message and made it to the port, several having completed part of the journey on foot. Frixos somehow managed them through the desperate crowds of people seeking escape from the island on that overburdened ship. Finally, it sailed for Greece and from there the AFS students flew on to the United States.

At the same time, the four

*AFSers had their fun moments too in the 1960s such as the 1966 Valentines Party in Madrid, Spain.*

Turkish Cypriot students were facing similar dangers and obstacles. Two of them were in the south and saw no way of crossing into the northern sector. The problem was solved only by the personal intervention of the newly arrived American Ambassador, William R. Crawford.

He appealed to the President of the Republic for a safe conduct through the lines, received it instantly, and arranged for a United Nations escort to deliver the two students to Doghan. The other two students were located and all four, with Doghan's assistance, boarded the first

Turkish ship that called in the north. From Turkey, they flew on to New York.

The next year, 11 Cypriot students came to the US but upon their return in 1976, the AFS program was suspended. It remained inactive until Wes Fenhagen, USIA cultural attache and former WWII AFS ambulance driver, was assigned to Cyprus in 1982.

He wrote to AFS in New York and suggested that it reevaluate the status of AFS Cyprus, and in 1983 the program resumed. Juan Carlos Correa, then regional director for Africa and the Middle East, visited

Cyprus and arranged a meeting of AFS supporters. Having applied to the U.N. peace-keeping troops, they met in an old hotel in the Green Line section of Nicosia. They appointed a Greek Cypriot Chairman and a Turkish Cypriot Vice-Chairman and set up one official committee for AFS Cyprus, with U.S. Embassy staffer Christina Hadjiparaskeva as the volunteer Program Coordinator. AFS Cyprus is in business again, still a triumph of ideals over ideology.

**R.A. Jellison**, former director of the US Information Service in Cyprus, and

**Juan Carlos Correa**, AFS staff

# The Rhinesmith Years: With Proper Training 1964-74

Stephen H. Rhinesmith brought the AFS organization just what it needed -- youth, problem-solving ability and training skills. Rhinesmith was 29 years old when he was selected as the third President of AFS.

An Americans Abroad returnee from the summer program to Germany in 1959, Rhinesmith had travelled extensively as a consultant with the Peace Corps and the A.I.D. (Agency for International Development).

He holds a Ph.D. from the University of Pittsburgh Graduate School of Public and International Affairs and is an expert in cross-cultural communications and group-training processes.

As Bill Orrick puts it in his unpublished history of the first 30 years of AFS, "It seems remarkably fortunate that AFS should have found a President so trained and with such experience at the very time when its primary need seemed to be reorganization, fresh motivation of volunteers, and staff training."

Rhinesmith indeed felt appreciated. "One of the greatest acts of faith in young people and in the whole purpose of this organization was the fact that a board of directors had enough faith in a young person, and in young people in the world, to turn over all of the assets and everything that this organization is, to somebody who basically had nothing going for him, other than youth, enthusiasm, spirit, some sense of management and a lot of international experience," he said.

He began his 10-year term by reorganizing and restructuring the staff. One Friday, he announced that 75 jobs were being eliminated. However, 60 others were to be created on Monday and anyone could apply for them.

The result was to streamline the US operations by reducing duplication of tasks. Job descriptions were written, and salary ranges and scales were developed, which made the staff feel more professional.

The Multi National Program passed from being a pilot into a full-flegded program option in 1972, and the Domestic Program came into being in the US, Italy and Switzerland, providing students with a home or work experience in a different socio-economic, ethnic, racial, geographical, religious or vocational situation in their own country. The year 1972 was also the beginning of the Soviet teachers exchange for AFS as the American Friends Service Committee, which started the program in 1961,

*Stephen Rhinesmith and friends.*

turned it over to AFS.

The AFS International Council was established, and had among its members Morris B. Abram, US Representative to the U.N. Commission on Human Rights; Leonard Bernstein, composer and conductor; Kingman Brewster Jr., President, Yale University; Edward W. Brooke, Senator from Massachusetts; Jacob Javits, Senator from New York; Dr. Rudolf Kirschlaeger, Foreign Minister of Austria; John L. Loeb Jr., investment banker and civic leader; Dr. Margaret Mead, anthropologist; Frank Pace Jr., former US Cabinet Member; and Marietta Tree, former US Representative to the U.N.

The Rhinesmith era was marked by its emphasis on training. At Rep Conferences and the annual Organizational Development Workshops for US staff, he led people through the process of first being trained and then feeling confident to train others. District Reps and Chapter Presidents learned how to write workshops to meet their own needs, to be creative and even go beyond the guidelines emanating from staff in New York.

This empowerment led AFS volunteers to feel more professional about their role in the organization. No longer is every counselling problem referred to a staff person; Chapter Presidents and Student Family Liaisons can be trained by their peers in problem-assessment techniques or continue their training and become

Diagnostic Counselling Reps.

While Rhinesmith agreed that from the volunteers' perspective, the emphasis on training and developing skills in management and counseling were most important, he felt that computerizing the financial structure made the biggest difference for the international operation of AFS.

Before the computer, it was impossible to know how the fees were determined. When they finally were able to compute costs on a per student, per country, per program basis, the national organizations could have an

enlightened discussion about the philosophy behind spending the money, not just argue about where it was spent.

This was a most important part of the internationalization movement. Volunteers and staff began to understand and participate in the decision-making process. They could see how a goal like diversity of socio-economic backgrounds had a financial component which might compromise or jeopardize the viability of other programs.

At the same time, Rhinesmith worked on clarifying the agreements between AFS

*The USSR-US Educators Program, begun under Rhinesmith, brought Emma Khomenko into this New Jersey classroom in 1972.*

*Making a birthday banner for President Gerald Ford filled the hallways at AFS, according to Doris Wilkins, a long-time staffer who now works in Publications.*

International and the network of national volunteer organizations and national offices. The same emphasis on volunteer and staff training that marked his tenure in the US prevailed at annual Regional Conferences around the world.

With all he was able to accomplish, he doesn't miss the presidency. "No, I did it," he said. "I'd love to go back and see everybody, speak at a World Congress or something. I gave everything I had to attend to the problems I saw -- to affect change. Somewhere between 5-10 years is the right time to lead

any organization, and I left when I had done all I could.

"What I really remember is the speeches, being out with the kids, the mid-winter weekends, the C.W. Post and Stanford University orientations. It was an extraordinary experience to lead a world organization. The great gift it gave to me, at a reasonably early age, was to learn to deal with responsibility and to be at ease with world leaders.

"I remember meeting the President of Austria. I walked down the halls with the red carpet and the gold doors that opened one after the other and I thought,

'What am I doing here?' But, it was a real opportunity to grow. It also gave me fulfillment, so that when I finished AFS, I finished climbing career ladders. I didn't have to prove myself anymore; and at age 37, when I resigned, I said if I had gone down in a plane the next day, I would have had no regrets."

Rhinesmith and his family, now living in Pelham, New York, hosted AFS students Indra Januar from Indonesia in 1982-83 and Lisa Dixon from Australia in 1984-85. "It was good, our kids are now 16 and 12. We couldn't host until I left the presidency," he said, "because of AFS rules. I think that the pressure on the student, staff and family would be too great if the President were to host, so we waited."

"Of all the experiences I've had, being an AA, working in Onward Travel during the summers, volunteering in a local chapter and being a host parent," he reflected, "the best was being president. I didn't have the kind of life-changing, mind-boggling experience in my summer as an Americans Abroad student or in our personal hosting experience. But, I had a peak experience as president that's equal to the best experience a kid has."

*Above: Rhinesmith lends a hand. Below: Rhinesmith is accompanied by two Austrians and a Dutch guitarist. Nur Pelit, the National Representative of Turkey, and Trustee Josef van Ranst look on.*

## AFS Is Love (And Marriage)

Many people take AFS very seriously. Consider the story of the van Holsteijn family in Ede, the Netherlands. When they decided in 1980 to become a host family, over the objections of their 17-year-old son Ed, it was near the end of the family-finding season. AFS in the Netherlands offered to let them choose their student from the papers in the office and they chose Carla, a sweet girl of Dutch descent from Urbandale, Iowa, again over Ed's objections.

Once in the family, Carla and Ed realized that they weren't meant to be brother and sister and told their parents that when they had chosen her as their AFS daughter, she was destined to become their daughter-in-law! Not the purpose of AFS, says Carla, but a nice fringe benefit!

Christine Souders told me a slightly longer story involving Sue Inui Kelly (former AFS staffer originally from Youngstown, Ohio) and her cousins from Galena, Illinois. It's hard to know where to start. Sue Inui was an Americans Abroad student to Denmark, and her family hosted a German boy named Helmut.

Meanwhile, her Aunt Franny and Uncle Tommy hosted an Indian girl on the farm in Galena. Their daughter Ann went on AFS to Sweden and later Ann's sister went to Europe to work. She met Helmut, now a law professor, not knowing that he had lived with her cousins in Ohio, and eventually married him.

Since we like happy endings, here's another one about a student whose natural parents were divorced and whose host mother passed away after the student returned home. In the ensuing

## Ode to the Student Selection Process

What kind of student should
   we choose
to send across the sea?
A super jock or passive miss
or one that's just like me?

A smiling face, a soulful look,
so many types we see.
A bashful boy, a six-foot girl
and some that pay full fee!

And then we have that awful
   choice
to make all on our own,
A Finalist or Guaranteed,
or should they ALL stay
   home?!

**Sally Hermans Burdick**,
host sister, host mom,
Chapter President, Area Rep,
parent of AA to Germany,
starter of 14 chapters, bus trip
and overseas flight chaperone,
and eight-year staffer,
currently Manager of Student
Selection and Placement

years, the AFSer saw his natural mom marry his host Dad.

And, just so we remember that it pays to stay involved, AFSers Maryse Pierrel and Niels Mikkelsen never met when they were both in the US (she in Corona, California, and he in St. Louis, Missouri) but when they returned to Europe in 1971, they got involved in AFS France and AFS Denmark, respectively.

They met at a French National Assembly in 1971 when, at the invitation of Bernard Lesterlin, National Director of AFS France, Niels came to promote the Inter European Progam. Maryse admits to using every AFS excuse to keep in touch with Niels. She called to compare notes about programming for students and attended the Danish AFS Language camp two years in a row, ostensibly to learn how it was run!

Married in September 1975 with many AFS friends in attendance (including Maryse's younger brother from California), they moved to Copenhagen. In 1977, Maryse was elected to the Danish AFS board and served for six years. Her last position was

chairperson of the committee that organized orientations and language camps for Year Program students.

Niels' career in government led him from the Ministry of Environment to the Ministry of Public Affairs to a three-year stay as the First Secretary of the Danish Mission to the United Nations. Meanwhile, Maryse has been working at AFS in New York. Before heading back to Denmark with their two children, eight-year-old Jan and five-year-old Louise, they will take a two-month tour of the US and Canada where all but two stops are AFS-related.

"I know that AFS has given me a lot of friends and a way to personalize events in other countries," said Maryse, "but best of all, it has given me a husband and two bi-cultural children which makes our family much more interesting than most, more challenging, but I think more rewarding."

M. E.

*Maryse Mikkelsen could have told Costa Rican Ginette Soto (left) and Kiwi Bridget Ikin that Danish grammer is nothing to smile at!*

*Bombay AFSers meeting with a Guru at a Hindu temple in August 1972. Along with the Americans Abroad students, Joan Trusty, Carolyn Brehm, Helen Mohrmann, Susan Regas and Brenda Malone, is Indian Returnee Satish Tibrewala from 1967-68 and some host family members.*

# Even the Pope Blesses AFS!

AFS Americans Abroad and Multi-National students who had spent a year in Italy were given seats in the front row at a Vatican gathering of 10,000 pilgrims from all over the world. When Pope Paul VI entered, before dealing with religious matters, he gave his "special word of cordial welcome" to the AFS group. The unexpected papal address resulted in a five-column article in the Vatican newspaper.

According to the AFS office in Italy, that space and the size of the headline are quite unusual. "After the audience, many people came to us to find out what was our special relation with the Vatican that had caused such an open endorsement by the Pope," said Roberto Ruffino, the Italian AFS National Representative. "God knows ..." The Pope said:

"A special word of cordial welcome goes to the group of high school students of AFSAI, who wished to be here, this morning, in order to greet the Pope before returning to their home countries.

"We trust, dear young friends, that your year here in Italy may have been a positive experience for all of you, and may have shown you the possibility of peaceful coexistence between different cultures: They may all gain from being open to one another and, although they all stick to their own originality, they may -- through a healthy confrontation -- better understand this living mystery of God's creation, man.

"Now that you return to your home countries, feel responsible to make your peers more sensitive and aware of the need of greater communication between nations, and thus build a more peaceful world -- a world more respectful of minority rights and more conscious of human richness as it is displayed by our different cultures.

"A proof that all this is no utopia, but rather an ideal that waits to be implemented, is in front of your eyes, here, although on a different level: You can witness it here in Rome, where people of all races and cultures meet to worship together, each in his language and according to his traditions, the Son of God given to us for the salvation of the world.

"As we think of Him, the perfect Man and the example of what mankind shall be one day when love has made us all brothers and sisters, we bestow our apostolic blessing on you, your families and the members of the organization that has brought you here."

**AFS World Review,**
November 1976

# Infectious AFSitis

In 1978, my sister left for Australia on AFS after having known of the organization for only three months. She was the pioneer in our family. That summer, we hosted four bus-stop students. This was the first of many groups we've hosted over the years. The experience of getting to know the students was so exciting that as a sophomore, I ran for President of our high school chapter and held that position until I graduated and went abroad myself.

That same summer, my cousin was visiting us from Michigan and became equally excited about the organization. The following year, her family hosted an AFSer from South Africa and my cousin became president of her chapter as well.

My year abroad was 1981. When I returned, having been opened to the world and its people, my family hosted a summer student from Iceland. At the same time, my cousin left for Mexico and her family hosted its second student, this time from Venezuela.

While in Guadalajara, Mexico, my cousin met and fell in love with a Swedish AFSer, but was separated from him at the end of their year. A year after her return, her brother left for New Zealand on his AFS year.

We have all been profoundly affected by this wonderful program -- it will have an impact upon us the rest of our lives. My host parents and my sister's have visited our family here in Rockville, Maryland, and we're still in touch with our Icelandic brother, as are my cousins with their brothers. My brother Eggert is hoping to return for a visit this summer, as we all hope, someday, to return to our "other" homes. Our families are that much larger and richer from these experiences.

With all that this has meant to my family, the most lasting effect will take place this September when my cousin marries her Swedish love. They have kept in touch since they left Mexico and each has visited the other. In fact, Peter, the groom, came to the States to study for a year in a college in Pennsylvania. He didn't care where he went as long as it was as close to her as possible!

My sister and I will be bridesmaids at their wedding. It's such an exciting feeling to be a part of this new family being formed. A new generation of AFSers will come from it and contribute to bringing the world a little closer, as I hope we all have, and will continue to do throughout our lives.

**Jenny Pratt,** Rockville, Maryland-Ecuador, 1981-82

*In the Van Alstyne family of New Jersey, AFS has played a part in the lives of three generations, from David (a WWI driver) to Joan (Johnson), host mom in 1977-78, to an Americans Abroad granddaughter.*

# Hygienic Horrors

I applied for AFS, and in the back of my mind I thought I would go to Germany or France, Italy, possibly South America. But I tell you, Sri Lanka never crossed my mind.

In fact, I remember my father saying to my AFS interviewer, "Give me a list of the countries. What's this country here, Srigh La-anka?" We decided that it must be one of the emerging African nations "And, ha, ha, Nancy," he quipped, "you'll probably end up going there."

Well, his ha-ha's became real about six weeks later, when I got this rather large envelope and sure enough, Sri Lanka was my destination. I remember my mother went into complete panic; no one knew where it was and didn't know that it formerly was Ceylon. She called the public library and pleaded: "You've got to help me. My daughter is going to spend the summer in Srigh La-anka and we haven't the faintest idea where it is."

And the woman helped her pronounce it right and told her it was Ceylon. So Mom went to her encyclopedia, and there were pictures of people riding elephants.

I got on the plane and proceeded to take a five-day trip to Sri Lanka, and my memory gets cloudy (this being 13 years

later). When we landed in Sri Lanka, and I had been travelling for days, probably in the same clothes, I can't even remember. I was dirty and exhausted. I had seen so many different things; my senses had really been combatted with all kinds of different sights, smells and sounds. I just wanted to lie in a coma for a while. And I pretty much passed out on the spot.

I met this family -- a mother and father who had an arranged marriage, two daughters, a son and an aunt. They lived in a really nice home. The father was a proctor, who in the English legal system prepares the case that the magistrate argues. They took me by car to their small estate (which looked pretty large to me), about 25 miles southeast of Colombo, the capital, and I went to sleep. They woke me for dinner.

They led me into the dining room. We sat down at a table, with all kinds of servants running around, and they passed me all this food, and it looked like chop suey, but I looked down and thought I'd see maybe chopsticks or a fork and knife. No dice -- they ate with their hands. Fine with me, but I was so tired, I had no idea *how* they did this, so I was literally playing with my food.

I had rice all over my mouth. I remember they asked me all sorts of questions, and I don't remember what I answered, I was so tired, and all of a sudden, I swallowed something that exploded. It was incredibly hot and so I reached for what I thought was a glass of water and swallowed that down and -- agh!! -- it was fermented coconut juice, a liqueur called "Akrak."

I thought, "I'm going to die, please let me die right now." But I didn't. And they kept laughing at me because my arms were covered up to my elbows in rice

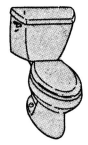

and curry.

Not only did I eventually learn the etiquette of eating this food, but I also built up a tolerance for spicy foods. Everything was a curry -- there was chicken curry, fish curry, meat curry, there was curry curry. And breakfast, lunch and dinner, it was pretty much the same. But the food wasn't the only adventure. Especially at that time, they kept looking at me with great bewilderment when I was eating.

I used both hands, and they used only one, the right hand, to eat. They said that the left hand was reserved for "hygienic reasons," but it didn't concern me until about two weeks later when I found that my supply of toilet paper had slowly dwindled and my tissue had disappeared. And I asked, "Can we have some more toilet paper?" They looked at me and told me that they didn't use toilet paper.

Well, I was 17 years old and didn't want to admit that I didn't know something, so I started to collect things such as paper from school, leaves, (banana leaves in particular, but I had a bad accident with them and couldn't sit down for a while after that) and I kept wondering what's going on here, how do people do it?

But, again, being 17 years old, I was not going to admit -- I mean, how can you ask somebody something like that? Well, finally, I reached the point of no return (I think it was right after the banana leaf incident).

I pulled away the second daughter, with whom I shared a

bedroom. She didn't like me too much because I was so hot (we're talking 120 degrees, 100 percent humidity) and I wanted to sleep under the fan and she got cold. I'm from Wisconsin and I tried to tell her about cold, but since they had never seen snow, they were really mesmerized by pictures of all this white stuff.

Anyway, I pulled her over and I said, "I've got this problem, I mean, you don't have any toilet paper and, I mean, what do you do? And she said: "Tee-hee, tee-hee, you mean, you don't know? Have you seen that bowl in the bathroom? That's a douche bowl and you're supposed to use it."

"OK, what do you mean?"

"Well, you fill it up with water and you wash yourself."

"What do you mean, do you sort of throw it up and splash it around?"

"Well, you just wash yourself."

So here I am in the bathroom, confronted with this great dilemma. I have this bowl, I have the water and I have a floor and a toilet, and I don't get it. But, I fill up the bowl, and there's no towel, no washcloth, nothing. So I just sort of threw the water up and it went all over the floor.

At the house in Hornau, I was confronted with a bidet. I didn't know what that was either. I turned it on and thought, what a clever little footwash, because we wore thongs a lot and I had to wash my feet often. But when I remarked on the neat footwash, they said, "That's a bidet." And since I didn't know what that was, I looked it up in the dictionary. So, the next day I said, I'm going to try this, enough of this throwing the water up and wondering where it's going to land. I straddled the wonderful little bidet, turned on the water, and I want to tell you, I thought I sterilized myself.

I jumped off this thing, the water was pounding the ceiling and it was so hot and I wondered again if I was going to survive the summer.

By the way, I solved my problem: I used to visit all the Western hotels and steal the toilet paper out of their johns.

School was a drag, I thought, at least when you have to go to school in the summer and its 120 degrees and your elbows are sticking to the wooden slats while wearing this horrendous uniform. The teachers used to come in and lecture from their old high school notes (which was easy for ancient history since nothing had changed. However, current history really was in the making).

I was priveleged enough to go to a rather fancy girls school. A lot of diplomats' daughters went there and I was friends with a few of them. Consequently, I met the Prime Minister of Sri Lanka, Bundar Nika (her husband was the Prime Minister who was assasinated in the '50s and she took over), and I met her son and I met a former president.

This was in the summer of 1974, during the time of the Watergate hearings. I went to an engagement party and I stood out as the only fair-skinned Caucasian. On my way there, some vagrant (from the lower caste, high on beetle nut) spit a great red wad on me and shouted, "Yankee, go home." This upset me but I went to the party anyway and found myself in a conversation with the former president of Sri Lanka. He said to me, "I understand your president is in a bit of trouble." "Well," I responded, "if he is, our system's foolproof in the sense that it will catch any misdeed that's going on." And he turned to me in all seriousness and said, "It's not easy to run a country, you know."

I met some nice people, but they were all the privileged people. I made it a point to go around Colombo and went from cricket clubs to some of the worst areas of the city. When I was in the country, I had a lot more freedom and, to the dismay of my family, I went in the back woods and saw how people were living, how they built their homes, transported their goods, bathed in side sewer sections, drew water, planted rice (and then pounded it for flour).

I used to see how men hung out at tea boutiques, which were no more than shacks, and they sold coconuts, cigarettes (fags, as they called them) and some sort of chestnut things that people used to eat. I got a really good feel for an economic climate that was so different from my own.

I mean, in the United States you pop the bread in the toaster. Not in Sri Lanka. There the people use open hearths and pots hanging, much like Colonial times in America, over fires fueled by coconut shells -- and this was a "modern kitchen."

One of my favorite stories is "meat tenderizing." You buy the meat from the butcher. It had been hanging out on a hook and it's got every imaginable thing crawling on it, and so to sanitize the meat, you boil it. But first, to tenderize it, you throw it on the floor and walk on it, then you throw it in the pot. And of course by then, it's like shoe leather, so you use spices and tenderizers to make it edible. After seeing this, I never wanted to walk in the kitchen again.

I used to have cravings for American foods like a Big Mac and a Coke. You could buy Coke -- they had a distributorship -- and when you were dying for Coke, you'd do just about anything. But it tasted different, bizarre -- sort of flat and sugary -- and I never could get quite used to it. Also, I ate 40 different kinds of bananas -- short ones, long ones, fat ones, hairy ones, brown ones, red ones, green ones. To this day, I rarely eat a banana.

To summarize, I would say that my summer in Sri Lanka was one of the most difficult things I've done, and because it was difficult, it was challenging, and when you're challenged, you learn. I learned a lot -- about how other people live, about a different religion, about an island full of people who not only didn't believe in Jesus but didn't believe in God!

They had no such concept. They believed in Buddha and the teachings of Buddha and that's very different from the Judeo-Christian ethic of the West. That was very interesting and I tried very hard to learn and appreciate Buddhism, almost to the point of trying to accept it because I was trying to accept their culture.

I learned about economic hardship and to appreciate where I come from, to appreciate what has been given to me, because there are so many people who don't have enough. We have so many resources, both natural and human, great diversity and freedom.

Sri Lanka today is caught in civil war, which hurts one of its primary industries, tourism. It's a beautiful gem of an island, but the people can't accept one another, and they can't give one another personal freedom. They're hampered by things such as caste that we don't have.

I learned how to share emotion, to put myself in somebody else's shoes and see myself, and my background and my country from a different perspective.

**Nancy Newald Stall,**
Whitefish Bay, Wisconsin-
Colombo, Sri Lanka, Summer
1974

## *Tug of AFS*

*Winter Program students at play during a 1971 weekend conference in Clinton, Iowa.*

## Transferrable Skills

Pleasant, forthright and sincere, Barb Kurtz seems like a normal 30-year-old. But, she's not.

Growing up in suburban Whitefish Bay, Wisconsin, the fourth of nine children and the third of four girls, she needed to establish her identity in both family and school. By her junior year of high school, she was involved in the Student Council. "I wasn't a star, merely a wholesome, good kid and yet I knew, even as I was involved in school organizations, that there was a bigger world out there. That's what made me want to be an AFSer. I certainly wasn't the cheerleader type, but I was outgoing and interested in people," she says. No doubt these attributes led to her selection as an AFS summer program student to Costa Rica in 1973.

"In Zaragosa, Costa Rica, there were chickens running around in the yard and my sister and I walked the 'backroads' [paths, really] to the dairy farmer to get milk that had never seen a bottle," she recalls. "The 'town' of Zaragosa had only a church, a puperia [sundries shop] and a bar. The mail was dropped off at the Rodriguezes house down the road and if you really wanted anything, you had to go to Palmares, the larger 'town' about three miles away. There were three other AFSers in the area that summer, but I didn't get together with them too often. I spent a lot of time with my host family visiting."

The family was small by Costa Rican and Kurtz standards -- only five children -- and loving. The father was a coffee farmer and a member of a cooperative so the family lived relatively well. The house had running water (available for showers only at certain times) and electricity for luxuries such as

a TV. "I can picture Maita [the mother] making tortillas and I had never seen a stove like they had. The kitchen was 'rustic," to say the least." The family accepted Barb and loved her as one of its own. "We still correspond and we've traded visits over the years. My real mom and I went and stayed with them for a good two weeks, and in 1981 two of my 'brothers' came to Milwaukee," she adds.

Barb returned to Whitefish Bay, graduated from high school, adjusted to the amenities of modern life and went on to nursing school. She chose nursing for what she considers pragmatic reasons -- she needed to study something so she could earn money. And, although she is a self-described "people person," by 1981 she felt her job in a cardiac care unit involved caring more for high-tech machines than for the patients. The frustration with her job and chronic travel fever led her to apply for an

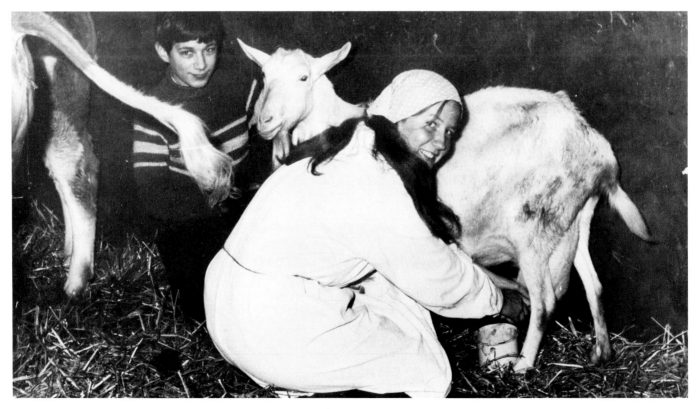

*Like Barb Kurtz, Joan Williams learned about milk that hasn't seen a bottle. She spent 1972-73 with the Greis family in Austria. Photo by Ernst Tatzer, Mistelbach, Austria.*

overseas mission of American nurses. What a change: from a modern hospital to a refugee camp in Thailand. "This was nursing. Hands on, using-all-your-senses nursing," she declares. There were no machines, there was a language barrier and there was Barb. "I was trying with all my senses to understand the people and their pains," she explains.

Her AFS experience became useful. "The skills I learned in Costa Rica in a sense equipped me to go further," Barb says. "I guess I had an advantage over the other nurses. The experience I had with my Costa Rican family prepared me for more intimate involvement with the people we were caring for." The American nurses were dependent on the orderlies and medics, mostly Hmong young men who had learned English, to translate. Barb learned a little of their language but she was most drawn to maternal/child-care nursing. She had discovered what she wanted to do -- midwifery.

Becoming a nurse/midwife required some ingenuity. In 1983, Barb left for another "cross-cultural" experience, this time a year in midwife school in Jackson, Mississippi. As part of a federal grant that underwrote the cost of her training, she then spent six months living alone in Vicksburg, Mississippi, practicing nurse/midwifery at a hospital that needed her services. To someone who grew up in suburban Milwaukee, Vicksburg seemed very foreign. "Vicksburg is a rural city. The people are friendly but the whole area is like a developing nation. Very poor," she says. Yet she felt the six lonely months were not too high a cost to bear for the skills she acquired.

In Barb's nurse/midwifery practice today, she feels that she is performing a much needed role

*Australian Rhonda Graham spent the summer of 1982 in Tak, Thailand.*

for many young mothers. Right now, she is on sabbatical to finish her bachelor's degree in nursing and, now married, may take some time to have babies of her own. Her interest in public health and maternal/child care will probably take her back to school for a master's degree and, if possible, she and her husband, Dr. Joe Layde, may take a year abroad for him to continue his studies and Barb to work in midwifery.

Technology, or the lack thereof, figures strongly into Barb's world-view. Her direct, intimate way of dealing with

people meshes with her training and love of "hands on" nursing and is a natural outgrowth of her roots. "Each time I went on another of these adventures, the building blocks were there: stable, positive experiences like growing up in Whitefish Bay and wanting to explore the world beyond," she explains. "The skills I learned as an AFSer are the ability to become close to people and willingness to try new languages. And the way I see it, my skills will be needed anywhere and everywhere, and language will be no barrier."

**M. E.**

## All This for Nine Hours in Thailand

Patty Shaner thinks the old saying "too soon old and too late 'shmart'" fits her to a tee. The former National Director of AFS Thailand and Peace Corps volunteer in Belize, Central America, is now 76 and working again for AFS in New York, this time to determine family placements and collating Americans Abroad applications.

She got involved with AFS in the early 1950s when she invited a German girl (hosted by the Von Briesen family) to speak to her Brownie troop. Patty decided then and there that AFS was an organization she'd like to join. The Shaner family went on to host a student, and Patty eventually became the Area Coordinator of AFS in Milwaukee from 1962-70. About three months after her husband died in 1970, Patty applied for the job in Thailand, sold her home and began a two-year stint as National Director in a country where she couldn't speak one word of the language.

Upon her return to Milwaukee in the fall of 1972, she volunteered at the Laubach Literacy Center, saw friends and family and then applied to be a bus-trip chaperone that summer, hoping that there'd be a seat available on the AFS charter to Thailand when she got to New York. As luck would have it, there was, and Patty boarded the plane with just her purse!

After a 27-hour flight (including a three-hour delay on the ground in Tokyo) they arrived in Bangkok around midnight. Patty called one friend, pleased that she remembered the Thai word for "telephone," and felt confident that she could direct the taxi driver to get to her friend's house. They had time to shop for a clean dress for Patty to wear and to purchase a gift for an AFS friend back home.

*Victor Laus (left) and Ho Hun Mun, Returnee Presidents for the Philippines and Malaysia, respectively, at a Bangkok conference in 1969.*

The charter crew could have had 12 hours' rest, but opted to fly after only nine to make up for the delay in Japan. So it was back to the airport to catch the charter home so she could work at the incoming student orientation at C.W. Post before chaperoning a bus to St. Louis. With all the crossing of the international dateline, she must have lived about five days in 60 hours!

M. E.

# AFS Roundup in Oregon

Pendleton is situated in the rolling country with wheat fields near the Blue Mountains and the Umatilla Indian Reservation in northeast Oregon. All conditions are right for a wonderful weekend when all the AFSers who spend their year in Oregon or Southwestern Washington arrive. The community donates 70-80 tickets to the AFS for the annual Pendleton Roundup, following a tradition started by long-time AFS volunteers Tom and Vera Simonton, and then offers marvelous hospitality to them and the 15,000 other people who attend each year.

"The roundup, or rodeo, is the coming together of the ranch people," explains Julianne Sawyer, Pendleton Chapter President. "It's not serious like Thanksgiving, it's more fun-oriented, to let your hair down after working hard all summer. The people around here raise sheep and cattle and horses, and when you have that combination, you get a rodeo. Even our community college has a rodeo team which does pretty well in the national collegiate rodeo competition."

It's a special roundup for the

70 or so AFSers, too. Since this takes place the second full weekend in September, it's probably their first time to see AFS friends since orientation in New York.

They arrive on Thursday and see the rodeo and Indian village on the rodeo grounds during the afternoon and then go back after supper for the "Happy Canyon Pageant," which traces the history

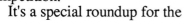

of the land and its settlement. The evening ends with a dance featuring traditional cowboy music.

Early Friday morning, they attend the Cowboy Breakfast in town where the AFSers usually sing or do a dance (a variation on "sing for your supper!") and then stay to watch the Westward-Ho Parade. There are no motorized vehicles in it, only horses and horse-drawn carriages. The local Indians walk or ride in full ceremonial dress and the AFSers are often treated to a Big Tom (Simonton) caricature of the rodeo, parade or themselves.

"They all love it," bubbles Julianne. "We send 'em home higher than a kite!"

*AFSers seem to love cowboy hats. Above: the students who had just come from the International Horse Show on their bus trip in New York State. Below: A grin as wide as a cowboy hat.*

# One Heart Full of Love

Luis Giminez came to us from Pilar, Paraguay, with limited English. With the help of six other volunteers, I organized a daily tutoring session and we took him through the Laubach adult literacy reading materials from September to December 1981. He was a very responsive pupil and was able to "fly" on his own the second semester.

I can still see him in the middle of the classroom with his tutors around him during a special Christmas party they organized. The present from the group? A big, wide cowboy hat that matched his grin. It seems they all had picked up on this fond wish during conversations.

His host family, the Osborns, supplied the cowboy boots which kept his feet warm during the Minnesota winter. He was so grateful for every kindness extended to him during the year.

On the last day of his year-ending bus trip, he wrote me a postcard to share what was happening. After the last talent show, his group of 41 students and their chaperone went to a room.

Holding hands, they started to talk about their feelings. "It was so wonderful," he wrote, "because we were 42 persons from 29 countries in one heart so full of love." It seems he learned English pretty well.

**Millicent Hanson**, Chapter President, Winnebago, Minnesota

*For all their hard work, AFSers do appreciate their Chapter Presidents and faculty advisors. Here, in Hobart, Indiana, Fernando Garcia of Mexico and Robyn Bashford of Australia present a certificate of thanks to their faculty advisor, Dorothy Thompson.*

## Bring Back Belete!

In 1982, the whole town of Hudson, Ohio, held a parade to welcome their AFS student home for his 10-year high school reunion. The student, Belete Muturo of Ethiopia, calls it a miracle that he even lived to see that day.

Belete was a very popular student when he lived with the Phibbs family during the 1973-74 school year, recalls Jean Colvin, former Chapter President in Hudson. That year, while his own country was going through the turmoil of revolution, he was learning of democracy in the United States. When he returned home, he knew he would become a rebel. Indeed, during that first year back, his life changed dramatically: He completed his high school education at the John F. Kennedy school in Addis Ababa, and stayed on to teach junior high for about five months.

He joined the National Democratic Party, which he felt was moderate, and worked

underground with it for about six months. Then, as he became more opposed to the direction of the government, he joined the rebels and went into the country to fight openly.

"I was arrested in November 1977, held in a highly secure prison for political prisoners, unable to contact even family," he recalls. "In the first three weeks, I managed to smuggle one letter to my host family. It cost me everything I had, which was about $6, and I told them where I was, and asked them to tell my parents and I also gave them the name and address of my girlfriend, who was one-month pregnant at the time. They started communicating with her and during the time I was in prison, my host family helped to support my girlfriend and child, sending about $25 a month and clothes.

"After I was in prison for about five years, there was a government amnesty that released about 860 political prisoners. Until then, I was sure I would never be released. About 400 of

the rebels from my group had been killed, so I was lucky to be freed, but then I was unable to get a job because all was controlled by the Communist government. I married that girlfriend and finally saw my four-year-old son, but I was still not 'free.'

"I was harassed almost daily. 'How do you earn your money?' they would ask. They threatened to send me to a work camp or back to prison for being a parasite on the society. When I got the letter from the church, it was a big 'freedom' and I carried it with me for the three months before we left the country."

The church he referred to is the First Congregational Church of Hudson. The Rev. Phibbs, who had since moved to a congregation in Pennsylvania, appealed to the church Overseas Mission Board to sponsor Belete as they would a missionary. Months before they figured out how to raise the money to bring him to the US as a student, they sent a letter offering to sponsor him and enroll him in an

*Kevin O'Hare of Dubuque, Iowa, had his own experiences in Ethiopia in the summer of 1972.*

*For most AFSers, the 1970s were a happy time. Here is the annual gathering at the White House with President Richard Nixon.*

engineering program at a nearby university. Armed with that piece of paper, he was able to persuade the government that he really was going to become a student and was allowed to leave Ethiopia to return to Ohio.

Since his return in 1982, Belete and family have moved to nearby Akron. The relationship with his host family is still strong; when his wife had twins last fall, his mom Dawn came to be with them. Belete is now studying economics with an eye to further education in law or public policy, useful knowledge if, and

when, he returns to Ethiopia.

"What is really in my heart is that AFS changed my life; it helped me to develop the concept of democracy and the struggle for democracy," he states.

The love of his host family is a tribute to people caring enough to get involved. "It was a miracle that I was able to come back and give something back to the community. AFS and the Hudson High School had time scheduled for me to speak at assemblies to the students and I'll never forget how they all helped to raise money to help resettle our family.

"Even Sabine Wille from West Germany, who was the other AFSer at Hudson High school in 1973-74, heard about my problems and sent money and clothes to our family," he adds.

The homecoming parade was the town's way of showing how everyone is involved. But it served another purpose: It offered Belete a chance to thank the community that may have saved his life.

**M.E.**, story from Scott Ramey, who was at Hudson High in 1982. Scott, who went to New Zealand on AFS, is now on staff.

45

# Different Tongue, Same Flour

I'll never forget the first night with my Argentinian host family. I arrived with minimal Spanish ability and maximum exhaustion. The family arranged a banquet for about 20 relatives so I could meet them. At dinner, one of my mother's brothers wanted to say something to me. I could understand only a small part of his message, but I think I got the jist of it.

Then, to my amazement, the family turned and looked at me. My mother asked if I understood what he said. Well, I thought so. I mean, I could understand a few of the words and I was trying really hard to follow the conversation. And then they started laughing and said, "How could you? It was Italian!"

Later that summer, my AFS sister and I were making papier mache. She brought out a bucket of water, strips of paper and some white powder called "farina." I was surprised to see a special powder just for papier mache so I quizzed her, "What is it?"

"Farina" she replied.

"Yes, but what's it made of?"

"Wheat. It's ground wheat. Don't you have this for baking in your country?"

Then I realized the "farina" was just flour. I was expecting everything to be new and different, a total learning experience. I'd say the packaging threw me off because it did; but really, I learned something new: to get the most out of my summer on AFS, I would have to look for similarities as well as differences.

**Robbie Weaver,** Camp Hill, Pennsylvania-Argentina, Summer 1980, now living in New York City

# AFS Favoritsm at Stanford

When I came back from my year in Finland, I attended Boston University for two years and then I transferred to Stanford University in Palo Alto, California. I have reason to believe that there are more AFS alumni per capita at Stanford than at any other school in the country!

Every time I wore my dilapidated AFS sweatshirt on campus, people approached me with the stock AFS questions: "Oh, where did *you* go? For how long? Do you know _____? She/he went there, too." Or, "My AFS sister/brother is from Finland," etc.

I asked the Dean of Admissions about his "AFS favoritism." He said that returned AFSers are always automatically high on his prospective list of applicants.

**Kelly Spencer,** host sister 1978-79; AFS Club President; and American Abroad from Brookfield, Connecticut, to Turku, Finland, 1980-81

*Talk about confusing! This boy's t-shirt says -- in French -- "Kiss Me, I'm Japanese."*

## Twice Sisters

This doesn't happen to everyone who has an AFS sister, but mine is going to turn into a sister-in-law! I was a host sister to Blanca Herrera (Colombia-New York '78-'79) and I am now engaged to marry her brother! The long arm of AFS reaches out. Our whole family went to Colombia over Christmas 1980. Her brother was in charge of entertaining me!

I went to Bolivia on the summer program in 1979. My host brother was the same age, and we were in the same class along with another AFSer from Minnesota. The school we attended in La Paz was divided into three sections, one where instruction was in German, one was in Spanish and the other was about half and half. I was so surprised to go to a Spanish-speaking country and realize that they expected me to learn German! I had been in El Salvador the year before to visit my sister who was in the Peace Corps, and we had hosted a Colombian AFSer so I was ready, I thought.

It's interesting to note that I experienced more hostility to being from New York than I did about being Jewish in a potentially anti-Semitic environment. My very first day at school, one girl commented how dirty New York is, as if I had made it dirty! My family took me to the cafe to see Klaus Barbie, the Nazi war criminal then in refuge, and although he was very heavily guarded, it was common knowledge that he would be there at a certain time each day.

I think that my encounter with the German immigrants to Bolivia helped shape my career direction. I am now pursuing a course that will lead me to be a therapist specializing in problems particular to immigrants, especially adolescents. My AFS experiences were fundamental in developing the cultural sensitivity needed for this work.

**Lois Indyke**, Long Island, New York

*It takes all kinds: An AFS Christmas card showing the different headgear of the world.*

# AFS
# on
# Parade

*The first place float in a recent Ligonier (Indiana) Parade during Fort Ligonier Days was designed by the local AFS chapter. The theme "Friendship Around the World" showed off the Americans Abroad returnees and the local Winter Program students in costume.*

*The Rose Bowl Parade, shown here in 1966, is still an attraction for AFSers. Jacquie Coppage of Pasadena, California, has been organizing annual AFS reunions since 1986 that draw hundreds of AFS supporters to the corner of Colorado and Orange Grove on New Year's Day.*

*AFSers on a Short Term Exchange from Williamsville, New York, marching in the Winter Carnival Parade in Saranac Lake, northern New York. Photo by Eleanor Sweeney.*

*Above: The second place float in the Claremore, Oklahoma, Chirstmas Parade was designed by the local AFS Club. Below: Gisborne, New Zealand, returnees on parade in Cook's Bay.*

# Tributes

*Even if you'd never seen snow before, you could catch the drift of these AFSers in Poughkeepsie, New York. Photo by Robert Niles, Poughkeepsie Journal.*
*Left: VIVA AFS -- a South American salute on skis.*

*William Dyal*

# The Dyal Years: Beyond Evolution to Revolution 1974-1986

Bill Dyal came to AFS with a strong background in the developing world.

For nine years, he was director of the Inter-American Foundation and had lived in Central America more than once. He had no history with AFS but immediately recognized its potential.

In challenging the global AFS community to internationalize its governance, de-centralize the programming and take its place as a leader in the field of intercultural learning, he had to take some risks.

"But it's not risk-taking for the sake of taking risks," he said in his departing interview in 1986. "It's the creative, innovative, imaginative reaching-out to cross rigid boundaries and the seizing of opportunities as they arise. I never saw internationalization as a risk. I thought it was the most natural thing in the world. And I didn't see program development as a risk. It seemed to me the only possible way we could go."

He has been labeled a visionary in large part due to his enormous faith in the people of AFS and their ability to overcome obstacles and change. "It is important to AFS to be a place where people dream dreams, and where dreamers are not put down by cynics. Vision is critical for us. But it is equally important that idealism be tempered with realism," he explained.

Known the world over for his enthusiatic speeches and warm smile, he visited more than 50 countries during his tenure and found ways to extend AFS programs to the People's Republic of China and India (countries whose combined populations comprise one-third of the world's people). In fact, his revolution started with these two countries as totally new programs that had to be designed.

This revolution is referred to as the "multiplier

*Bill loved going to the arrivals and departures, where he gave inspiring speeches to send the AFSers off.*

concept." For years, each individual student made his or her impact on the family, school and community, and the depth or intensity was largely dependent on the teenager's ability (and willingness) to effectively communicate AFS ideas of accepting differences and respecting other cultures and languages.

For the first time, programs were successfully designed for adults whose work was communication. Teachers primarily, but journalists, lawyers and artists, too, were chosen because they were professionals capable of transmitting the AFS message to larger groups of people over time.

Their programs are based on homestays and work experiences. Language training is offered if necessary, and the programs are more structured and focused than the programs for teenagers. Most of the new adult programs are multi-national, which allows participants to learn about many cultures simultaneously. For instance, British teachers who went to the People's Republic of China with a group of Americans commented in their evaluations about the chance to get to know some "Yanks" and dispell some of their stereotypic ideas about them as well as learn about the Chinese and their ways.

Dyal felt that AFS belonged especially in troubled regions. His recollections of one special night during his trip to South Africa in July 1985, printed in the AFS International Newsletter, give an insight into the man.

" ... That evening was so spectacular that only a video could really capture it all. The big AFS event was to have been hosted in the black township of Soweto by the chapter there, but because of the declared State of Emergency, it had to be moved to a white

neighborhood, Jabula Centre. But nothing was lost! Busses brought Soweto people. More then 400 people attended, roughly 55 percent white and 45 percent black. No one recalled ever seeing such a gathering.

"I entered in the midst of Soweto dancers and singers and a heart-stopping candle-lighting by a dozen mixed returnees. There was a speech by Timo Smouse, Soweto AFS Chairman and returnee. And, finally, a huge cir-

cle was spontaneously formed-- black and white, arm in arm, singing "We Are the World." It was a spirited night in AFS I shall never forget. And as everyone kept saying -- only in AFS is such possible in South Africa today.

"Nowhere did I hear anyone talking about whether or not AFS had a future in South Africa, only what the challenges and possibilities were ahead. We must not be blind to AFS's vision in such a climate."

*"Hand in Hand" by Michael Sandstrom, an AFS volunteer, 1974.*

*Many AFSers teach aspects of their cultures to their host families and friends.*

## Teaching Teachers

### 6 Feb. 1985

Ever since last term, when I heard that I would be teaching Chinese to two AFS foreign teachers, I had been feeling uneasy. In fact, petrified! I had heard that they could speak only a little Chinese and I could speak only a little English ... I had learned English for a few years, but I had never in my life spoken one word of English or Chinese to a foreigner. How would we talk? How would I give the first lesson? What would they think of me? And would I be able to learn some English from them? This AFS program was to be an exchange studying and teaching languages ...

Laurel comes from America. She seemed open and enthusiastic. I felt her sincerity from her voice and laughter. Janina comes from England. She seemed serene and gentle, endowed with a sense of humor.

Although I had heard that

## Chinese Changes

The People's Republic of China has been sending university-level students to the United States for many years, but since AFS developed its high school-level teachers program, many American families and teenagers have been able to interact with Chinese citizens, one on one.

Theirs is such an unknown country, so vast and populous that it's "mind-blowing," as the kids say. AFS teachers who go to China, like Peter Labouchere from England, find people staring and asking lots of questions. He realized that he was the first westerner to ever visit some of the places he arrived at by bicycle or bus.

When the Chinese teachers come to the US, they are also stared at and asked questions. When I met a group of Chinese teachers at an AFS conference in Des Moines, Iowa, in 1986, I was struck by how "American" their clothes looked. Flannel shirts, blue jeans and sneakers are not exactly what I pictured as Chinese attire. But they said clothes were very expensive here and of course all their clothing was made in China.

Not too many years before, in 1982 to be precise, the first group of 12 teachers came to the United States wearing their navy blue "Mao" suits with white shirts, each carrying a suitcase identical to the others with identical contents within. Imagine the rate of change they are facing as they seek to diminish the gap between communism and capitalism.

AFS staff member Carol Byrne, who works with the Visiting Teachers Program, explained that of the great land mass that is mainland China, most of it is unarable mountains or deserts. Agriculturally viable land is at a premium.

No wonder a Chinese teacher who was living in Topeka, Kansas, couldn't understand why we (in the US) spent so much time and money on our lawns, growing grass we couldn't eat. It wasn't necessarily a criticism, he said, just amazement.

**M. E.**

foreigners have a taboo against talking about their private affairs with strangers, I was amazed and delighted to hear them chat about their past, marriage and family on their own initiative. And with sincere interest, they inquired about our common interests ... the distance between us was shortened quickly ... With their little Chinese, my little English and plenty of assistance from facial expressions and hand gestures, we made ourselves understood.

On this same day, I was walking with Janina when Laurel suddenly turned and asked me in Chinese: "Ni shi shen me yen ye shou," meaning "What kind of animal are you?" I was unable to make heads or tails of this. Was she saying I was an animal? Miss Yang, a companion who was walking with Laurel, explained to me, "She asked you which zodiac animal you are."

I sighed with relief as I understood her mistake, and we all laughed heartily with the explanation ...

**7 May**

Translating literally can often get us into trouble. I have learned now how important it is to use and understand idiomatic expressions.

**3 July**

Each country, each nation, has its pride, has something to make other countries respect and admire them. Now, we all have an eager desire to know more profoundly the other country's history, culture, local conditions and customs. We realize that in order to have our wishes fulfilled, we must improve our language ability. Laurel and Janina are my English teachers and I am their Chinese teacher. All of us try to be good teachers and good students. We have a mutual understanding.

Excerpts from Diary of **Wu Yun-Ji**, Chinese teacher and English student. Reprinted with permission from the AFS Int'l Newsletter, Vol. 1, No. 4

*There is so much to discover. An American student learns the sitar from her Indian friend.*

# AFS Mexico: Coping with Crisis

Crises of different magnitudes happen everyday in AFS, according to Mary Ann Zaremba, the Director of Program Support for AFS International for 10 years. To see how an AFS network handled a crisis of the most serious kind, go back to the morning of Thursday, Sept. 19, 1985, when an earthquake rocked Mexico City, site of the AFS National Office and home to more than 10 million people, including 18 AFS students.

to ascertain that they and their host families were safe. By Friday, they managed to send a telegram to AFS International to let them know that the students were all right, but there was no way of knowing if AFS would receive the message. Being incommunicado with the rest of the world was immensely frustrating. The students worried that their parents didn't know they were all right and parents (rightfully) worried on their own along with the Mexican AFSers in the US and elsewhere. Fortunately, by Monday, a ham

callers.

As for the 18 students living there, after the crisis passed they gathered in the AFS office for a sort of debriefing. They talked about how they felt, what they had worried about and what, if anything, they might have gained from living through this.

"In group discussions," reported Program Coordinator for Mexico Jackie Craig in the AFS International Newsletter, "we learned that they were not at all frightened. Their major concern was whether their families knew they were all right. And they

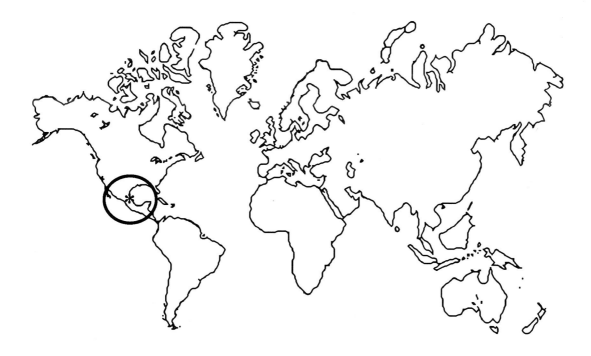

Communications were in chaos as the central station for long distance telephone calls was destroyed and the local lines were jammed by people trying to reach their loved ones in other parts of the city.

By the end of the day on Thursday, the President of the Board of Directors of AFS Mexico, a volunteer, had managed to contact all 18 students

radio operator assured everyone that AFS was indeed aware of their status.

Some parents, of AFS students in Mexico, but located many miles from Mexico City, panicked and created another layer of crisis, so it was important for AFS staff members to receive a daily briefing with whatever concrete information was available to offer the concerned

experienced the same frustration we all felt at not being able to help enough. All of them, with no exception, had helped in some way or another -- some preparing food with their host families to deliver to the homeless; some at school getting donations of food, medicine, clothing, blankets and other things; and some boiling and transporting potable water to disaster areas." **M. E.**

struggle for a visa.

First we tried to see if there was a Chilean consulate in Accra, the capital of Ghana. Foolish idea. Then, when we finally found an office willing to issue a visa, they looked at my passport and said it was all full, there was no room for the visa to be attached. At last I persuaded them to give me the visa on a piece of paper and staple it into my passport. I think I went through about two passports a year in that job!

**Juan Carlos Correa**, Regional Director AFS-LACAP (Latin America, Canada and the Pacific), formerly Regional Director of AFS-Africa/Middle East

# We'd Give You a Visa But ...

As a Chilean national residing in the United States but working with the AFS region of Africa and the Middle East, I found I was often the first Chilean many people had ever met. Some thought my name was Mr. Juan Carlos and never did use my last name, while others, when introduced to me, would ask if I was from Korea!

A big part of my work was trying to set up AFS in new countries (or re-establish it in places like Morocco and Cyprus). With all this travelling, I would be asked lots of questions, such as what was a Chilean doing, going from Egypt to Israel to Cyprus to Jordan? It seemed to me that the Americans would walk right through and nowhere was my life more difficult than at airports.

The worst incident happened when I was trying to go from Togo to Ghana. The border was closed by land, so the airport was always mobbed with people waiting up to six or seven hours for a simple 20-minute flight. We were trying to start an AFS program in Togo and I forgot to get a re-entry visa for Ghana (which I had to pass through en route to Kenya). So I began the

# Staff Perspectives

AFS has always had the enthusiasm of returnees fueling the program in their own countries. Encouraged by President Stephen Galatti, returnees throughout the world started their own organizations and had summer reunions, conferences and camps where they learned how to stay involved in the total AFS picture. It was young French and German returnees who laid the groundwork for the Americans Abroad dimension of AFS.

But youth does not mark patience as one of its virtues and there was tremendous turnover in the leadership of the returnee groups. Fortunately, there have been some who, as they got older and finished college, held on to become national chairmen or directors of the AFS offices in their countries.

Some current AFS International staff members, including Executive Vice President Tsugiko Scullion (Japan-Oberlin, Ohio 1963-64) and Vice President for Asia Don "Mohan" Mohanlal (Ceylon [now Sri Lanka]-Nebraska 1968-69), Director of Student Placement Regula Stamm (Switzerland-Kermit, Texas 1961-62) have devoted their entire working careers to AFS. Their value to the

*Tsugiko Scullion*

organization is immense, their perspectives on it unique.

"If you want to know about the internationallzation, just look at my titles," said Regula Stamm. "In 19 years, I went from being the 'Overseas Representative' to being 'National Representative' to finally, 'National Director.'

"Now, I have come to the International office to see what they do here that I couldn't do back in Switzerland. I find myself fascinated by the procedural accomplishments. In Switzerland, alone as a National Director, I couldn't have created the process to place almost 3,000 students each year as we do in this office."

Mohan has been a big part of AFS in almost every part of the world, as he moved through

*Don "Mohan" Mohanlal*

positions of leadership in his native Sri Lanka to Regional Director for Africa and the Middle East, to Vice President for LACAP (Latin America, Canada and the Pacific) and now to his current position as International Vice President for Asia. He lent his perspective to characterize the first four presidents of AFS. "Stephen Galatti was the entrepreneur, Art Howe was the administrator, Steve Rhinesmith was the professionalizer and Bill Dyal was the visionary and each has been right at the time," he said.

In a recent interview in Gateways, Tsugiko Scullion said she expected to work for AFS only for a few years, but "there has never been a dull moment." She started in 1972 as the Area Consultant for Connecticut, became Regional Director for Asia and the Pacific, then Vice President for EURAFME (Europe, Africa and the Middle East), served almost three years as Vice President for Program Services and was named in 1985 to her current position as Executive Vice President. "AFS has always been an organization which has kept both idealism and pragmatism in balance in meeting the challenges of a changing world."

*Regula Stamm now oversees a much more sophisticated placement department.*

# To Live a Life of Meaning

Letters from **Chiara Carcianiga**, Lecco, Italy-Mt. Horeb, Wisconsin, 1981-82, to M. E., her bus trip chaperone

*For some people, a year on AFS can be a radical awakening, a shaking up of all they have known and wanted. For others, it is a more natural, evolutionary step, new and different but less rocky. The letters that follow are from a clear and inquisitive Italian AFSer who loves walking in the mountains. Her name, Chiara, means light.*

## Easter '83

Spring has come to Lecco and I am feeling very well now. I had quite a boring time during the winter months. I don't think I can enjoy winter at all. Now I have come alive again -- I ride my bike always, I hike and climb, I have a very good time with my friends. I wish I could talk to you about the mixed feelings I have -- I do like my hometown and I realize every day that my friends are the greatest gift I ever got from life; I'm graduating this year, but I can't STAY in Italy and go to university here after high school for five more years!

I think I'll get back to Wisconsin sometime in the future, but I will probably go to South America and work there first. I'm keping in touch with my Mt. Horeb family, and they want me to go back. Of course, for me, Wisconsin has not become a fine goal or ideal to strive for -- I don't usually idealize places.

I don't want to settle down in *any* place yet, but I want to see my friends and do something with them in the future.

You know, I always wanted to travel and get to know new cultures...

## Christmas '83, Amazonas, Brazil

I got the last letter you sent to me because my parents sent it down here. I have been spending two months here already, working in an agricultural school. My job is to teach young people (in their late teens) how to write and read. Also, I have a few other jobs like taking care of plants, fruit and animals and the kitchen. Amazonas is a great place! Right now the climate is nice and sunny, people go around in shorts and t-shirts all year round.

## March '84, Lecco

Let's go back in time to that night of July 1982 when we talked about what I was feeling like and what I was going to do with my life ... My real fear was to become a person who runs after money and to become a slave of Western society; in a way I guess I felt like I was the one who had to decide for her life and I was afraid I would not be able to do it. I spent a whole year not knowing the answer ...

My first impression of Amazonas, of the population and life-style was so sad!!! People living in straw houses with mud everywhere you go. Not much in the houses -- just a hammock and a table and a few tin boxes to store food. In most villages there's no electricity and the water they drink doesn't come from a well, but they take it from the river where they wash things and paddle their canoes. I tell you, it was not easy to get to understand poverty, but after two or three months I started to really appreciate and "understand" and love this lifestyle.

The school I was working at teaches reading and writing up to a 6th grade level. They also learn how to work in the fields for their own family requirements (better and more varied diet) and in order to earn some money. All the kids we have (45 boys and 40 girls who come and go, alternated every two weeks) come from small villages in the forest where they wouldn't have the chance to study more than 1st grade because even the few teachers there don't know *THAT MUCH!*

I just loved my kids and I've learned so much from them. (I'm not talking as if I were superior because I'm not ... I don't feel like the holy missionary who makes miracles, I just learned so much ... and they gave me so much love ... gosh ... they made me cry so-o-o-o hard when I had to leave!!!) Of course, most of them are descendants of the native Indians, so their temper is calm and slow, they don't like to tell the truth and learn so slowly that sometimes I felt like I was teaching for nobody, but as time went on I felt more and more satisfied. I didn't get to see the original Indians who still live out in the forests, but I got to go into the forest for a whole week with my pupils' dads, and that was really something.

We people of the big cities think we can do and know so much, but we should be a little more realistic at times. We know how to survive only if we find a supermarket. We would die in the forest, eaten up by the mosquitoes. There's such an immense variety of insects and parasites ... it's just incredible. Living in an agricultural school, I even managed being a vegetarian (I've been a veggie for six years now) but I realize that it was just nonsense there. Man is still a total part of the cycle of life and death and is still so close to nature that being a vegetarian doesn't make any sense.

The main food is fish (huge fish ... it's unbelievable) and farinha, a flour which looks a lot like chicken food but which I became very fond of. There is so much delicious fruit. I loved it! This just to tell you that I didn't starve at all. People who live in the forest might have a wrong diet but they can always find something to eat. People who live in the slums in the cities like Sao Paolo are really starving and there's no way to get out of it.

The people who run the school are all very young. There are 13 of us, and Pe Augusto (a 54-year-old missionary from Italy) just left his job as principal/director in order to give a 28-year-old former student the chance to help his people. There's so much work to be done and Brazil is such a new country that you still feel like you're a human being and *this* is what life is all about. What frustrated me so much here in Italy and in the US was to be "a number." It's hard to

express it but I never accepted it.

My plans now??? I have to think a lot and take some time and reflect, but they already asked me to go back and be a teacher in one of the "lostest" villages in the forest. I want to learn something about medicine (being a volunteer in the Red Cross?) to be able to help more when (and if) I go back. Besides, I have many, many, many other things to do and I'm happy. I might even take some short courses here and there. I'm still living my AFS experience and taking advantage from it (more work with AFS in town, of course!!!).

**November '86**

This time I'm home and I will be staying around this area at least until July 1988, when I get through NURSING SCHOOL. Of course, this might sound new

to you, but I'm already attending my second year of school here in my home town, so that I can become a PROFESSIONAL NURSE, as we call them. This new interest got me when I was in Brazil for a second year. It was even more satisfying, but I realized that I could have done so much more if only I had known more about nutrition, health and nursing. It's a hard school: five hours working in the hospital (different wards) in the morning, four hours at school in the afternoon, plus studying at night for classwork and interrogation, for five days a week.

I've been learning so much ... but I've had to give up many other things and interests too. Of course, if I go back to Brazil or to some other developing country, this profession will help me get the visas and stay in the country.

*AFSers place a great emphasis on friends: Midyear Conference at Eastern Illinois University in 1982. Photo by Lisa Owens.*

## English is a Funny Language

His accent was strong, even at the end of the year when we met, so when he sat around telling stories, you could understand some of the words, but not all. He had a very gutteral sound for the letter h and said an r like a Bostonian.

One of his best stories happened at the beginning of the AFS year. One day, he came downstairs and smelled cabbage. He walked into the kitchen where his mother was preparing dinner and exclaimed, "Ooh! I love gahbage." His mother replied, not missing a beat, "Good, you can take this basket out right now."

Luis also had some other adjustments to make to American life. I don't know why, but many AFS stories are centered around the bathroom, and Luis told of his first shower in Illinois. He remembers having a problem because he asked for a douche, which caused a few strange looks, but when he got the idea across with pantomime, he was shown the shower.

Now, this was the situation as Luis told it to me. He was standing next to the tub and looking at the water spout. He turned on the water and it came out as if to fill the tub. "How was I going to get the water to go up and come down to be a shower?" he wondered. There was only one set of handles to turn on the water.

There were no instructions, and after standing for 10 or 15 minutes, Luis finally squatted down and splashed himself clean. (Later that week, he pulled aside his little brother and first swore him to secrecy before admitting he couldn't figure out the shower!)

And if any people tell you that they speak perfect English before

## Colorful Scribbles

Yellow chalk,
Pink chalk,
White chalk on green:
I can't read the words,
So this is what I've seen.

**Lisa Hill,** Hanson, Massachusetts-Japan, summer 1984

they come here, make sure they have learned American slang. Luis had another embarrassing moment when, needing an eraser, he asked his math teacher, "You know, I made a mistake. Can I please have a rubber?" Thank God for a sense of humor!

**M.E.,** from **Luis Santos,** Santos, Brazil-Winthrop Harbor, Illinois, 1982-83

## What Accent?

I'm the kind of person who easily mimics the accents that I hear. I can speak English like a German, Rhodesian or American from the Midwest or South. And, except for some slang and a few expressions, I never thought there was a language barrier between South Africa or Australia or the United Kingdom and the US. Really, we all speak English, don't we?

So, at one of the C.W. Post orientation sessions, you can imagine my surprise when I realized that one of the South African girls was "translating" what I was saying into English -- South African style. Then I saw

that there was a deaf student who depended entirely on reading lips. She couldn't make out what I was saying because of my Midwestern accent!

**M. E.**

## Accents II

Picture, if you will, a tall, blonde girl dressed "Western" with a cowboy hat and boots. Since I was the chaperone of her bus trip, I walked over and introduced myself. She replied, "Hi! I'm Bet-tina from De-en-mahrk!"

I couldn't believe my ears. There was no Danish accent at all.

"Where did you live this year?" I asked.

"Nashville," she replied, perfectly reproducing the southern inflections, "Why d'you ask?"

**Susan Ford,** host sister (whose first fight with her Norwegian AFS sister came when Susan got a lower grade in Senior English than her sister!), current staff member for the Northwestern US and a former bus trip chaperone

# Friendship Above Politics

With newspapers highlighting the continuing squabbles between the Arab and Jewish populations of the Middle East, it is heartening to know that two young girls, one Arab and one Israeli, became fast friends in a small town in California.

Howaida El-Said from Egypt and Ortal Zuckerman from Israel were both AFSers in Lodi, California, in 1982-83. "When we got to know each other," said Howaida, "we found we're not that different in what we believe, even politically."

Ortal added, "We know there are differences and we know we can't solve them. So we don't discuss it." Howaida further explained that a teacher had asked them to talk as representatives of Israelis and Arabs, but that they had refused.

Ortal agreed with Howaida and said, "We can't speak for our countries. We are people, not representatives."

According to an article from the Lodi News-Sentinel written by Lori Houston, the girls talked politics with each other once, and that was enough. But, even in discussing this while sitting on the living room floor of the home of Howaida's host family, Stan and Liz Rosenquist, some things were unavoidable.

Howaida tried to explain why she was not a representative of the Arab people in that her country recognizes Israel, unlike other Arab states. "But we do object to Palestinians not having a place to live," she couldn't help adding.

"Yes, but Howaida--," Ortal began, then caught herself and laughed. "I try to avoid politics."

The girls recalled an incident, certainly not a singular one, that surprised and deeply impressed them both.

A man unwittingly said to them, "You're from Israel? All right! I'm with Israel all the way. Hang the Palestinians."

"I was a little embarrassed," Ortal remembered.

"And I was shocked to hear that man say that," Howaida agreed. "But it did not affect my feelings for Ortal at all."

One of the many things both girls have learned -- from each other and from being in a foreign country -- is simply that things aren't always what they seem to be.

"You have a stereotype about people because of government," Ortal said. "But you get to see people as people and not as what country they are from. This is one of the successes of the AFS program. It doesn't matter where you are from after all."

Howaida agreed emphatically.
**Chica Maynard**, AFSWORLD
December '83

*Howaida El-Said (left) and Ortal Zuckerman.*

# Welcome Despite the War

Political events and international conflicts can place a certain strain on an organization like AFS, which keeps pointing to higher boundaries than those of nations. In the summer of 1983, during the Malvinas or Falklands Islands affair, I was at C.W. Post working as an orientation group leader.

The students from the United Kingdom arrived early on in the wave and were told that the Argentines would arrive the next day. I admit, we Americans wondered what would happen, hoping that there wouldn't be a problem.

We need not have worried. When most of the people in camp went down to greet the bus full of Argentines, we witnessed a most unusual event. A group of British students asked to board the bus and said, in unison, "Bienvenidos a los estados unidos!" (Welcome to the United States!) We Americans just stood by and cried.

**M. E.**

*An AFS Christmas card.*

# A Lifetime in Ten Minutes

Kitami, Japan
February 6, 1983,
2:40 to 2:50 PM

**2:40 PM**

A thin film of ice slowly forms in the glass beside me. Eight black-robed judges sit to my left, an interpreter to my right. Before us, four young athletes in the peak of condition and form move slowly in graceful tension. Their dinstinctive robes, belts and sleeves set them apart as skilled marksmen of Kyudo, the ceremonial and martial science of archery practiced in Japan, but rarely outside.

In this little city of Kitami, tucked far away in the frozen north of Japan, tension grips the entire rank of spectators, judges and newsmen. The only sound is the soft swish of the contestants' white-clothed feet slowly, exactingly moving to their appointed positions. The mounting pressure sharpens and my mind searches, almost in pursuit of relief from the tension, to what drove me to this crowded hall thousands of miles from home, numb with cold, immersed in an ancient culture, and now observing the spectacle of ceremonial combat.

Our son Matt, in his exuberant manner, came bustling home from high school barely a year ago and announced that he had applied to be an AFS student. He knew only that he had to compete with other applicants for a year's stay in some location far from home. We both felt pride and apprehension, but left the final decision to him. In a few days, he learned he was accepted, but the destination would not be fixed until just before he left.

We tried to foresee every obstacle, every problem, and haunted the mailbox for the fateful letter. When it finally appeared, it calmly announced that Matt was being sent to Kitami, Japan. The combined resources of neighbors, school and home began to generate information; we hungrily absorbed it and began to learn of the little logging and farming village near the north coast of Japan's northernmost island. It would be bitter cold, isolated and strange.

**2:41 PM**

My feet were like blocks of ice. The auditorium's bitter cold added to the sense of incredibility. Surrealistically, the line of Kyudo archers approached the invisible line from which they would loose their arrows. If there was any noise before, an utter hush now fell on the crowd. I was aware that my hands were breaking out in a cold sweat. Why was my son

Matt the very last in order? Couldn't they see how cold he had become? All of the other aspiring archers were dressed in white sweaters and longjohns under the traditional robes, but as a "Gaijin," or foreigner, Matt had not detected the subtle hints that contestants might ward off the piercing cold, provided nothing was said to the contrary.

**2:42 PM**

The first contestant had straightened from the deep bow of intense respect to the Kyudo masters sitting in regal, expressionless judgement. The second was starting the straightening-up process that seemed to take minutes, but was only in rigorous, controlled, slow motion. Five, ten, maybe fifteen seconds ticked by. My eyes darted sharply right. The targets were so very far away, so very small, so inconspicuous. I was used to the American archery target which for evermore would seem so huge, so close. The interpreter softly whispered in my ear, as the cold drove color from her face, "Watch each arm and hand motion, they are very important." She knew, even more than I, that family reputations, pride and social standing were being carried by the cream of Japanese youth in front of us.

My son, tall, incongruous and obviously not Japanese, was last in line, yet because of common dress and motion, began to fit naturally into the tableau before us. Each archer would shoot just two arrows. There was no need for more! If form were well executed, even the second arrow was somewhat superfluous. In the round of competitions that had preceded this last set of four young people, few arrows actually struck home. Not once had both arrows found their way

to the target. None had hit center. Even in the opening ceremonies, the deeply respected masters of the centuries-old art had failed to consistently hit the target with both arrows.

I vividly recalled Matt's lengthy and detailed letters of explanations, and long and mutually supportive telephone calls. He carefully explained that hitting the target was a vital part of Kyudo, but not the central concern. Instead, Kyudo focuses on the mind, upon self-control, so that the student of Kyudo learns to gain mastery over his own will and learns to submit to a higher calling. The devoted student fully explores the self and discovers how to tap the vast resources to be found in a thorough understanding of self; he learns to avoid the quest for a supremacy measured only by the figures on a scoreboard. Long, hard hours of agonizing labor went into each and every miniscule movement. During poignant and longed-for telephone calls, Matt would tell us a little of the aching, painful muscles, the seemingly harsh discipline for slight, forgetful transgressions.

Only later would I learn from his host parents the fuller extent of the labor and commitment Matt had invested in Kyudo. When his Japanese mother had described to me in loving detail the cost to Matt that this competition represented, even she was astounded at his perseverance. But, in deciding whether she would accompany us to this contest, she found the tension and suspense would be more than her usually stoic nature could deal with.

How would Matt fit into his new home and school? His big size, above average in his high school at home, would set him apart instantly in Kitami. The largest school uniform available, required of all students in Japan, fell far short of a flattering fit. The quick decision had prevented language training. The extraordinarily well-designed orientation provided by the AFS went a long way to help, but it was entirely in Matt's hands to make the exchange successful.

My mind flashed back to that day when our hearts and minds had reeled as we drove towards the airport on the eve of his journey to this beautiful land of forests and mountains. Would he be alright? What if he got sick? Or injured? Whatever would happen, Matt was now in God's hands. I clearly recalled the relief we suddenly knew, as we saw him off, that he'd be okay! He was embarking on a modern odyssey to experience events, encounter people and overcome problems that he would never forget. He was entering a phase that would become adventure only years

afterwards and in the fond retelling in which time would diminish the loneliness and struggle now so real.

**2:43 PM**

It had been incredibly fast, or was it an incredibly slow, two minutes? Time seemed to rush by, but hardly moved. The first arrow of the eight that would fly twanged into the framework around the target. A miss! Matt's two arrows, still gripped in symmetry to his body, would be numbers seven and eight. He had not moved a fraction of an inch, eyes lowered, body erect and firm. Would that moment of activity never arrive?

A small, discreet catch of breath marked the second arrow's flight into the other side of the target. Suddenly I became aware that the second archer had already notched his first arrow, and was placing his feet in a precisely defined pattern that had been decided upon centuries before. Now, abruptly, Matt moved for the first time since taking his place; a move so small I had almost missed it. The nearly invisible motion had transformed him into an ethereal image of evolving complexity and power. I suddenly realized that I was trembling. Was it the intense cold? I had to stop to gain control. I could not let anyone know how involved I had become.

And then it dawned on me like the rising sun: the expressionless judges, masters as high as Fifth or Sixth Dons, classes of expertise far beyond the coveted black belt, were not expressionless to promote fear. Never would they do that! Instead, their expressionless faces were the only mechanism they had to avoid all possible distraction. Each archer must be

free to perform to his maximum, total quest for excellence. I felt at one with each archer before me. The slightest sound or movement, the slightest, thoughtless attempt to encourage could only rob a contestant of his total absorption in his task of mastery: mastery of form, mastery of motion, mastery of self.

The third arrow, then the fourth were let fly. I now understood Matt's last instruction as he parted to his preparations hours ago. "Remember to listen, Dad. Listen for two sounds; the target seems to resonate. It sings! When the arrow misses, there is a kind of flat twang to the sound," he explained. "But the most important sound will be heard, or not heard, before the arrow hits." My confusion showed. His smile of gentle and loving knowledge, superior knowledge imparted from a master to a novice, lit the face of my 18-year old.

He went on, "You see, Dad, if the string snaps against the bow when the arrow is released, in time and usage it would fray and wear sooner than necessary." The serious student discovers that Kyudo expects perfection in keeping with the ideal of self-mastery, conservation of what is good, strong and beautiful. Twisting the bow in a fractional, measured twist in a split instant would prevent wear of the string. How could a human learn such dexterity, such absolute control? Was it even possible?

**2:44 PM**

The second archer had, with total possession of mind and body, turned to a sharply defined kneeling position behind the first. Now the judges had an unobstructed view to observe the skill of the third archer as he began to raise his bow. The arms moved into their most demanding chore, drawing the bow while high above the head. Slowly, as if pulling the world apart in a titanic surge of power, the arms began to spread. Muscles rippled, discreetly hidden. I took courage to seek Matt's eyes behind the third archer, but they had been carried by the precisely measured turn of his head to rivet on the target. His eyes would remain fixed on the target until the very end.

**2:45 PM**

I tore my eyes from my son in time to see the scorekeeper mark two Xs for two misses. The contestant's technique had been flawless; would the miss hurt his chances to make the passing qualification for First Don, or first degree black belt? My heart leaped in silent protest to the row of judges. The effort had been so beautiful, so perfect. Surely the misses couldn't stand against that magnificent display of courage and control.

My understanding leaped higher! How obviously true! To hit the target was important, without a doubt. But I was witnessing a spectacle that rivaled the most thrilling moments of theater. These athletes were vastly more than finely tuned machines hurling arrows in bunches to make a cheapening ratio of hits to misses. These magnificent contestants, in top physical form, in absolute control of a finely tuned mental attitude, backed by a thorough understanding of centuries of history, competed to demonstrate understanding as well as energy, skill and balance. These athletes controlled their efforts so absolutely that there was no need for noise, for grunts, for cheering mobs. My heart began to surge. I realized that my concentration had been broken and I had lost track of Matt!

**2:46 PM**

A solid, drum-like beat struck

me from the right. The slightest ripple of gasps, followed by a unanimous turn of the masters' heads, all signalled that an arrow had found its target. Involuntarily, my eyes sought out the arrow. Where was it? Ah, there, right on the edge, but on the target. A circle went up on the scoreboard and I was dumbfounded when I added up the marks: five Xs to mark five misses and a circle to tell us one arrow had found its goal. Number six it was! Six! Oh! Seven and eight were Matt's!

I jerked back to see my son. His powerful arms had risen to reach for the sun. The eight-foot bow reached high above his head, arms rippled with a surge of power. The string began to be drawn back. One arrow, rigidly held in his hand, the other drawing back inexorably, slowly, to the point of release. My breath stopped. His skin was like marble, beauty beyond belief. I began to master myself; my shaking subsided. I dared not let the slightest sound reach my son. I felt my face grow flat. Devoid of expression. My leg muscles twitched. My back screamed. I could hold out, but could he? Could he survive the awesome pressure and the agonizing physical demands? Every cell of my body cried out in support. I glanced at the masters; incredibly, I saw sweat forming on one of their brows.

That very morning, Matt had hugged me, saying, "Thanks, Dad, thanks for coming. After a year here, I was so afraid you might not make it." It's true, I had tried to schedule a visit six months earlier, but a sudden emergency thwarted my plans. But we were both overjoyed to see each other

again. I realized how ignorant I had been just hours ago. My mind began to flood with gratitude for the incredible honor that the judges, the masters, had accorded me in permitting me to sit in line with them.

After this experience, and whether Matt won or lost, qualified or missed, when this was over, I would plead if I had to, to bow in honored Japanese fashion to my son's faithful masters. These men had seen to the preservation through centuries of a priceless art, much more than a mere science, an art that would teach such incredible grace and power to my son, the son that I loved with all my heart. That supple statue of marbled power in front of me was the profound beneficiary of centuries of care, of expressionless love! But yet not at all expressionless!

**2:47 PM**

The next-to-the-last archer was now deep into the kneeling bow. This bow, I now knew, was much, much more than a mere convenience to permit the unobstructed viewing of how well my son had learned his art! It was a profound expression of respect and gratitude to the masters for their devoted labor in providing a forum for this spectacular display of skill, integrity and strength.

**2:48 PM**

My son continued his steady, sure draw. Would it ever end!? Raw power shone out like a searchlight with a startling burst

67

Raw power shone out like a searchlight with a startling burst of motion. The hand snapped back. My heart fully stopped! Time froze. I could picture each foot of trajectory. Quarter-way, half-way, three-quarters; had the sound of snapping string gone by? Could I have missed it? Where was it? Surely he could not have held that tension for so long, without a twitch, without expression. His leg muscles bulged. Time stood still. Would that arrow ever arrive? And then it sounded! My mind began to caress the sound, to analyze, to catalog, to compare. Yes! It was! A hit! A hundred gasps. The interpreter jerked, my head following, and there it was! The arrow stood straight out. Proud, noble and fair. Right on the innermost ring. The first one of the day! I was witness to a birth of manhood. I trembled with tension. I looked back quickly to Matt.

**2:49 PM**

Somehow, as if nothing incredible had just happened, Matt moved his second arrow into position. Again, his mighty arms started their reach to the heavens. If time had stopped before, it fully ceased now! The draw back continued. Back, back, the tip touched the bow, the arms started down to their final, appointed position. Not a sound, not one sound. The arrow flew. It missed! Incredibly, relief surged through my body. It was enough! He was human, he was still my little boy; a man, without a doubt, but still fallible. The hard-won skill, the intense pressure had not made him into a super-man. My knees jerked spasmodically as I tried to quench my own intensity. The judges visibly relaxed. My mind involuntarily reminded me that not once had it registered the twang of the snapping string. As

little as I knew of Kyudo, I recognized that there had been quality in Matt's performance.

As I watched with enormous fatherly pride intricately mixed with profound respect for a masterly performance, the tip of Matt's bow stopped a fraction of an inch from the floor. He bowed to the judges, then straightened as my lungs surged with the need to breathe deeply again. My voice had failed me and my eyes were damp from tears of joy. The urge to rush to my son nearly overcame me. But the slow-motion tableau had to be played out. Matt's powerful arms had lowered, and now he stood erect again, and in a graceful, measured, confident turn, he soundlessly slipped out of sight.

**2:50 PM**

The hush relaxed from rapt silence, replaced by soft murmuring from the spectators. By some unheard command, the hundred competitors hurried to form a single body before the greatest master. My son stood in the back row in tense repose. The group, in perfect unison, bowed. The spectators grew still. When the group straightened again, the master spoke, and the interpreter whispered these words in my ear: "Young students of Kyudo, look upon Matthew. They say he is 'Gaijin.' Perhaps so, it is not for me to know. Remember him well. Model after him. Learn his ways. Respect his skill. And so, like him, you will bring honor to self and country. Farewell." The master bowed to the students. I

allowed myself to breathe again.

The journey to the airport was quiet. A new master of Kyudo sat beside me. I felt the touch of his hand on mine, his shoulder powerfully against me. "Thank you, dear God," I said to myself. "My son is whole and well and you are in control."

\* \* \*

It has now been nearly three years since the events I have just described. Shortly after my son's stunning success in Kyudo, he completed his year of exchange in Japan, flew home to us and started his college education, planning a career in chemistry. Six weeks later, he and his mother, while passengers in a properly operated automobile, were killed by a speeding, drinking driver in Pasadena, California.

The draft of this manuscript lay untouched for two years. I could not stand to read it myself. I choose now to overcome the terror and rekindled memories to share with my beloved Japanese people the priceless gift they gave to me. Though decimated by the loss of both my wife and only child, I am the most fortunate of all men; for nearly 19 years, I was the father of Matthew, who grew to become a master of Kyudo. Few share that great honor.

**John McMillin**, father of Matthew, Pasadena, California-Kitami, Japan, 1982-83

*AFS volunteers, the Keenans (right) have scrapbooks filled with pictures of their AFS family, including pictures from their many summers as Dorm Parents at C.W. Post orientations. Below: There's a cross-cultural message in learning to eat popcorn with chopsticks.*

# The Eleventh Commandment: Honor thy VOLUNTEERS!

Since 1984, the Galatti Award has been given to ten outstanding AFS volunteers around the world. The award provides these dedicated volunteers an opportunity to gain new insights into the whole of the AFS organization by sending them on a specially designed trip, expenses paid, to share their expertise with AFSers in another country. The winners are:

1986 -- Rosi (Rosemarie Zirpel) Popp of Osnabruck, Germany

1985 -- Rosemary Gettleman of Cleveland, Ohio; and Rolf Neiger of Switzerland

1984 -- Lorna Clayton of Dundee, NSW, Australia; Eunice Grimaldi of New York; and Dr. Erich Langer of Rottenegg, Austria

1983 -- Elita Hawley of Salinas, California; Edith Baker of Auckland, New Zealand; Carlos Lazarte of Lima, Peru; and Gus Leimkuhler of Kansas City, Missouri

**Edith Baker** was recommended for the award by the New Zealand Executive for her breadth of AFS experience. She has served as a member of the National Executive, chaired the student logistics committee, established chapter development fund-raising, served on the national selection panel and was the Area Rep for half of New Zealand. Her 14 years of service have helped build strong programs for a strong national organization.

**Lorna Clayton** organized and runs the Orientation/Language Camps for AFS students to

## Starting From Scratch

Gus Leimkuhler went to Dublin, Ireland on his Galatti Award trip in March 1985. His mission was to help AFS Ireland develop a stronger volunteer base, an obvious problem given their dwindling number of host families. Gus brought two slide shows, one about how the Kansas City Area handles volunteer development and another showing what an AFS experience can be like for students

By the time he got to bed the first night, and long before he got near a slide projector, he saw how much work was needed. The head of the volunteers had picked him up at the airport and took him to meet his host family. They were very pleasant and welcomed him warmly, considering that when Gus left New York 12 hours before, a host family hadn't been arranged yet.

"That evening," recalled Gus, "we were sitting in front of the fire with a mug of hot tea to dispell the cold, and they looked at me and said, "So, what is this AFS?"

He leaned back and began at the beginning -- volunteer development, one person at a time.

Australia. Her book "When Do I Bow in Australia?" is a widely used resource (beyond AFS) that is sensitive to the needs of the newly arrived multi-national students who have little knowledge of English or the Australian culture. She's a resource person, excellent counselor to students and chapters and an asset to the New South Wales Hills Chapter, where she has been a host mother, counselling coordinator, publicity officer and vice-chairman.

**Rosemary Gettleman** started volunteering for AFS in 1963 by serving on a local family-selection committee. Now she is Area Rep for the 27 Cleveland chapters. She has led them through many innovations.

Cleveland was a pilot city for the Chinese Teachers Program, Summer Homestay Program and Inner City Exchange Program in addition to hosting and sending about 40-50 students per year. Her fortes are student counselling and administrative organizational abilities. "Working as an AFS volunteer, I feel as though I've picked up three or four graduate degrees in everything from management to human behavior," she says.

**Eunice Grimaldi**, an Australian now living in New York, has been an active AFS volunteer for 24 years. She was appointed by President Steve Rhinesmith to serve as the AFS' first representative to the Economic and Social Council of the UN and has been a Trustee and Director on the AFS Board. Known as a "walking advertisement for AFS," she has been part of the Departure Day activities on the West Coast for years and has always been available as a counselor.

**Elita Hawley** founded the Salinas chapter in 1956 and has been a full-time AFS volunteer since then -- just the kind of dedication her friend, Stephen Galatti, would have expected and admired. She oversees 19 districts with 67 chapters as Area Rep for the largest area in the U.S.

**Erich Langer** was an AFS student to the US in 1959-60 and has been active in AFS Austria ever since, from helping with student selection and counselling to raising funds, despite his own demanding medical career. He founded the provincial chapter of Upper Austria, thus setting an example in Austria for decentralization. In 1979, Dr. Langer initiated the AFS aid program for Southeast Asian refugees and organized language and other courses to help them adjust to their new environment. He is now working on establishing an AFS foundation for helping refugees.

**Carlos Lazarte** began his AFS involvement as a student to Ojai, California, in 1959-60. Fifteen years later, he became an AFS Trustee, working on the policy and international advisory committees. He has served as coordinator and Vice-President for AFS Peru and been a delegate to several AFS conferences. The General Secretary of AFS Peru recommended him for this award because of his strong support for new programs and breadth of understanding of the international scope of AFS.

**Gus Leimkuhler** has always been primarily interested in the students. A librarian at North Kansas City High School, he has been an enthusiastic faculty advisor, host parent and Student Selection Coordinator for his chapter and has been a Diagnostic Counselor, Area Counselling Chairman and Area Administrative Chairman serving the Greater Kansas City Area. He has also been a bus trip and class exchange chaperone and a delegate to a World Congress.

**Rolf Neiger** was an AFSer to California in 1963-64. Years later, he was still involved in AFS Switzerland and served as Chairman of the Swiss National Board from 1980-85. He is known for his outstanding teaching and training skills, and his attention to detail.

**Rosi Popp** came to the United States in 1950 as part of a group of 111 German and Austrian students paid for by a US State Department grant. After her year in Tenafly, New Jersey, she returned to Germany filled with enthusiasm for AFS.

At a reunion during the summer of 1951, she remembers telling Galatti, "We Germans know about your country ... but so many Americans don't know about ours." These young returnees wanted to organize an exchange for American students to become AFSers, too. Galatti told them to "just go ahead and DO it."

Rosi went around Germany finding the 50 families who would take American students to start the Americans Abroad program there. Now an Area Rep and member of the Osnabruck AFS Committee, she has done just about every volunteer task: recruiting, interviewing, organizing chapters, training volunteers, hosting, fund-raising, chaperoning summer program students. In the mid-'50s, she toured the US with Galatti to speak about AFS. As she said in an interview recently, "The basic grassroots work the volunteers do is still so important. They take care of the human needs, the relationships. Things happen, yes, things change, and that part is still the same."

*Here's a couple of happy volunteers!*

# Here's Arizona

The AFS volunteers in Arizona plan a full calendar of events each year and at the end, says Tuscon Area Co-Rep Nanette Cosart, "We feel they really know Arizona." Eight years ago, the volunteers began to organize three major annual excursions for AFS students, families and volunteers. "Some of us thought the AFSers should see the Indian area," she said.

These trips are mandatory for the students, some of whom resist at first but never regret it. Host siblings are encouraged to come because it's a great way to get them involved and the limited spots for adult chaperones are so coveted that there's a waiting list!

The main trips are a four-day excursion in November to see the Indian Reservations; a February legislative weekend in Phoenix, the state capital; and a family overnight to the Grand Canyon in June. In addition, in January the Tuscon area students go to either Douglas, on the Mexican border, or to Morenci, a mining town near the Gila Mountains.

In November 1986, the Field Operations Consultant for Arizona, Jean Wine, joined the trip to the Indian Reservation. Her report follows:

"Our group consisted of 23 students, host siblings and adults. Travelling in a caravan of cars, a van and an RV, we kept in constant contact with each other via CB radio. AFS volunteers prepared wonderful meals. Our first night was spent at the Tuba City Boarding School, where we were treated to various displays of Indian culture. The students had a unique opportunity to socialize and exchange ideas and addresses with their Indian contemporaries.

"Later, we visited the Hopi Reservation, where we toured an electronics factory and visited the tribal offices. During our visit, we

AFS Chapters around the United States have included Native Americans in their programming. Rudy Minster of Sheboygan, Wisconsin, sent this photo of Domestic Program student Kirsten Cross from California, Indian guide Michelle Pringle of the Stockbridge-Munsee Indian Reservation and Winter Program student Mark Devereux from Australia.

attended a discussion by Patrick Dallas, director of Hopi lands, regarding land disputes between the Hopi and Navajo peoples. We spent an evening with Navajo honor students at a school in Chinle, where we learned to prepare Indian fry bread. The evening ended with a communal meal and songs.

"The next day, we climbed down into Canyon de Chelly, an incredibly spectacular spot with beautiful vistas and quiet solitude. In the distance, the Navajos could be seen tending their sheep. After visiting the ruins at Canyon de Chelly, I left the caravan, so I could visit Globe, a small copper-mining town with a 25-year AFS history."

Although the itinerary changes slightly each year, the AFSers always go through Sidona and

Oak Creek Canyon (famous for its red rocks). Once, the AFSers were at Ganado College during a "Pow-wow" and saw the ceremonial dances. By organizing these encounters with the Indians of Arizona, local AFS chapter people have grown in their understanding of the different cultures in their own backyards. The AFSers themselves benefit, too.

M. E.

# The Wild Hog BBQ

The Aransas Wildlife Refuge at Austwell, Texas, is widely known for the whooping cranes that nest there. For the past three years, it also is known to AFSers of southern Texas as the home of the "Wild Hog Bar-B-Que." It started when the manager of the

refuge, the late Frank Johnson, was an AFS host father to Win Trisk of the Netherlands.

Win loved the refuge. He was allowed to hunt wild hogs and deer and whatever else was available, skinned the animals (he arrived knowing how to tan skins) and sent the skins back to Holland.

Now, every November the fall AFS orientation is held at the refuge. It's a weekend which culminates in the famous "Wild Hog Bar-B-Que." The men in the chapter, schoolteachers mostly, go out to hunt the hogs. They build a fire out of mesquite wood, and roast the hogs on a spit -- little ones that are only 50-60 lbs. It seems that some of them can get up to 450 lbs.

What made this a memorable event the first year has not become a tradition, thank God. According to Southern Texas Area Rep Martha Bernhardt, Win convinced the teachers to barbeque one little 20-pound hog whole (not quartered). When it

was done, they placed the head on a platter in front of an Australian boy who was there on an exchange weekend from Houston. Then, to everyone's disgust, he and Win scooped out and ate the insides of the head (eyes and all). As Martha said, she couldn't watch all of it, but at least it was cooked and not runny!

**M. E.**

# Growing Up in Uruguay

*James de Gregori of Houston, Texas, went to Tomas Gomensoro, a small city in northwestern Uruguay, from February 1983 to January 1984, where he lived with the Ramos family. They have three children, exactly the ages of James' natural family and the father is a veterinarian. Thanks to James' mother, Gayle, excerpts from James' letters home follow:*

### March 8

You better treasure this letter, it's the last one in English. All is well here. The Ramoses are extremely nice and loving. Kissing the cheek is part of every action (including a bath). You kiss both parents when you enter, leave, wake up, go to sleep or anything else. My lips are going to be permanently puckered.

We have two houses. The

smaller one in Bella Union is really cute. The front is his veterinary office, the back is the house. The entire backyard is a grape orchard, also with lemon and grapefruit trees -- which all make incredible juices. Steak is an everyday, every-meal thing here. The meat is incredibly good, so tender you can cut it with a spoon.

We eat a small, family breakfast, then after working a bit, we go and do whatever we want. Lunch, the main meal, is in series: soup, then the main platter (meat), then the vegies, and finally dessert (usually of fruit). I know why I never liked coffee in the States -- because I never tasted South American coffee. On my first day here, I crossed the river into Brazil, where we shop (it's cheaper there). There aren't any customs until a while into Brazil ...

Dr. Ramos has a huge collection of old things of the gauchos (cowboys). He also has an incredibly huge skin of an Argentine boa -- it's about 15 ft. long and 4 ft. wide.

The gauchos are every bit as romantic and poetic as they're supposed to be, (granddaddy would love it). They haven't changed a bit. They carry knives in their belt, wear baggy pants, smoke self-rolled cigarettes and wear flat gaucho hats and drink mate´ from a gourd. The bar where the gauchos hang out is hilarious. It looks like one in a spaghetti western. The horses are tied to posts out in front. . .

Fabian (the brother my age) collects beer cans, and Pablo, who's the same age as (my own brother) Roger, has a couple of fish tanks. Is that incredible?

The only night life is dances, which last all night. When people go out, they go out at 10 PM and don't return until 5 or 6 AM. The rivers are wide and clean. There are eucalyptus trees everywhere. There are also ostriches. Maybe I got Australia after all ... Please send the following: all those books, a permission to travel outside the country and to ride Pablo's moped, my transcript and transfer, film and your love.

## March 11

Soon, I will start school in Bella Union. I have to get up at 6 AM and be in front of the secondary school in Tomas Gomensoro at 7 AM to catch the bus to Bella Union. I study from 8 AM- 12:30 PM. It seems that this is not much studying, but it's not true. There is no Phy Ed, no lunch and no electives. I have six subjects, all difficult, all scientific and mathematical, with the exception of "English". ... I have many friends in Tomas Gomensoro. During the day, we play basketball, soccer and other things. At night (on weekends) we go to the club to play cards, pool, listen to music and drink beer. We don't drink much beer because it is not against the law and is not a vice. In Uruguay, there is much respect for the law ... Send me a good photo of the family. My family cracks jokes when I show them the photos of my dogs and my girlfriend -- but not my family!

## March 23

I've made about three times the friends here than what I had in the States. Close friends here put their arms around each other and when you see a female friend or meet a new one, you kiss cheeks. Some of my friends remind me of my friends in the States: there's a Jack, a Mark, a Ric and a Steve and even a Roger (Pablo). I'm known as "Importado," "Terror de las hormigas (ants)" because of my big feet, "Yankee" or

*Another side of South American AFS--Peruvian volunteers, mostly returnees, reviewing applications for AFS in 1967.*

"Hames" (Spanish pronunciation of James). Here, jokes are not taken seriously. Some of my friends are Gringo (he's Italian), Bocha (big head) and Gordo.

I've become totally non-racist, non-prejudiced and have learned to accept faults in everyone, for God knows I'm not lacking in faults.

**May 29**
One of the important parts of my experience is that I learn about Uruguay, but just as important is that I get another perspective of the US. Believe me, people think differently here about the "Red, White and Blue." One of the big heroes here is President John Kennedy, and they even have a stamp with his picture. People here really respect our democracy, but are against our policy of intervention in countries in a revolution, such as Central America. . . The US was called the "Papa Buena" but that's changed to "Papa Mala" with Republican politics, especially in Central America.

**July 1**
Has anything changed there? I didn't think so. Well, if you all haven't changed, at least I have some. But you'll have to wait till January to see that. Did you know there are practically no drugs in Uruguay? There's a bit in Montevideo. Here, nobody could get them if they wanted them (which they don't). There is plenty of drinking, although less than in the States.

**End of October**
I have had a very full weekend. Friday, I went to the club, as usual. Saturday, at 6 AM, I went with a friend, Ariel Rodriguez, to his ranch to shave sheep. We went on horseback to bring in the sheep for shearing and the cows for milking. I

brought in a herd of sheep alone (about 150). That gives you an idea of the intelligence of sheep and cows, when they let one man (or one Gringo) drive a hundred of them around. It's incredible the bales of wool you get from one sheep. We killed one, too, and cooked it on the open fire for lunch (yummy!). The gauchos are the best part; they're witty and fun-loving. They can strip a sheep at full speed and laugh and talk at the same time. After lunch, we rested a bit, drank mate´ and talked some more.

At 2 PM, I went to a reunion in the church. I'm in a group of "Solidarios." Our goal is to rid ourselves of "egotismo" and selfishness, and try to help others. Sounds corny and b.s., but it's good. The rest of the day was filled with the "Pericon," the gaucho dance (which I participated in, riding a borrowed horse and wearing borrowed hat and outfit). Then a dance with an orchestra and dinner at 11 p.m. A full day.

**November**
Sorry I haven't written, but right now I belong to Uruguay, but when I get back, you'll get 101% of me returned to you.

**December**
I just got back from a wonderful weekend in Artigas (the city). I stayed with an ex-AFSer that went to Missouri. She wrote a poem about how important it is to be human.
I personally don't have the slightest droplet of prejudice left in me. Prejudice is a form of ignorance.

**January**
I love you always Butch, no matter how many times I threatened you to maintain my superior position as big brother and no matter how many times

you sold my records or knocked down my beer cans to impress your friends or rebel against me. Those immature little fights are behind us now, the stupid jealousies that made us fight over *who* was going to invite Stevie (now Steve) over to spend the night, and *who* could outdo whom in sports are gone. We've got only the future and I'm sure it'll be a future of sharing, friendship and support.

# Unhappy Birthday
Since 1982, when we first hosted Lilly Bohorquez from Ecuador, my family has been very involved in AFS. I was the Club President for two years and my parents were Chapter Presidents and really got AFS going in Butler again. In 1986, they decided to be a host family again, and did so for a Sri Lankan boy.

By the time I was supposed to graduate from high school, I had been on Americans Abroad to Oberthingau, Germany, and had met so many people from all over the world through AFS that I was reluctant to leave for college. Fortunately, I went to the University of Wisconsin at Oshkosh, where there is a strong Model United Nations program (which attracts many other AFS returnees).

There is only one thing I don't like about AFS. The students always depart from our area at the end of June (on or very near my birthday). I can't remember the last really happy birthday I had because I'm always so sad over losing a brother, sister or friend. I guess I can live with it though, because I love the rest of the year!
**Sue Ellenbecker**, Butler, Wisconsin

## Beautiful Flowers

With a final skid-grind, Pan Am flight 188 was in Nairobi. My Pan Am flight, my window-seat and my movie screen were in Nairobi. I was in Nairobi. I was "home." Smoking is now allowed. Applaud for the pilot. It's been their pleasure to serve me. Please fly Pan Am again. I was in Nairobi. I was "home?"

The exit-parade is forming but economy class will follow clipper class which will follow first class. Thank you. Do I need my down jacket? New York had a blizzard. Excuse us, we're taking Molly's picture. Smile at the stewardess. God, does she wear the makeup.

I'm finally at the door and I actually have to walk down runway steps? It's completely backward here! No, I don't need my gym shoes shined and yes, a dollar is cheap for a genuine fertility doll. Sir, I realize my passport picture looks funny but what did you say was wrong with the visa? Then may I have it back, please? Thank God the bags made it here. Oh damn, I forgot my coordinator's name. Who's supposed to pick me up? No, I don't need a taxi and quit eyeballing my camera. I think my ride's here but what the hell's his name? Ernist, it's Ernist. "'Jambo' Ernist," I greet him, and I learned 'jambo' in my Swahili handbook. I didn't want to be completely in the dark.

"Hello to you Mark and welcome home," he says. So, this is Nairobi. This is home. No, I really don't mind driving through a game park in a Jeep. Does it have lions? My flight over was wonderful, thank you and only twenty-six hours airtime. No, they served chicken and spongy potatoes. Well, spongy means they were bad like garbage only not quite. No, Kenya isn't much like Ohio. Oh, you've

misunderstood me, I do like it here. I think. North Olmsted wasn't too exciting. I needed a change. High school was deadly! Go Eagles! I've had it up to here. Is it much further to the hotel? I know I talk fast. I'm sorry. It's the Figtree Hotel and they don't have a swimming pool? They have hellish sun and no pool. No, I'm not mad, surprised is all. Yes, Americans are very funny people.

Ah, the Figtree Hotel at last and I didn't see a lion or an elephant. They have me sharing a room with a Tasmanian guy. American Field Service thought of everything. He's going to ask me questions about football. I hate football. Why did he bring a knife? Would you get a look at this knife. This guy's a happy camper. They do have running water here, don't they? Yes, Americans are funny people. Damn, there's a million mosquitoes in here. My house had better have glass windows. That usually keeps out bugs. I'll have to tell them that at the desk. What if the family lives in a mud hut? I'll kill myself and go back to North Olmsted. They had better speak English, too. I mean, I hope they speak English. Where is that hideous music coming from? What should I say to the family when they come? Hello, I'm your American host-student, smile and handshake. God, that sounds stupid. "Jambo, habari zenu?" Did I say that correctly? I'm sick. What if it's malaria? Take one chloroquin tablet weekly. I did that already.

"It's nice to meet you, Steve," I say. "Ernist tells me you're from Tasmania. Oh, you hunt mostly kangaroo. I see. You play Australian-rules football and you want to know how to play American football too. My family picks me up in the morning, and you? Well, what's a 12-hour bus

trip when you've already come this far? I have 15 on this arm and nine on the other. I hate mosquito bites. I'll talk to you in the morning."

My host family is here and I haven't said good-bye to Ernist. "Jambo family." I'm American. I mean I'm in your family now. Thank God they speak English! Yes, a trip to the market before we go home would be fine. Would I like papayas? Actually, I've never had one before. Sure, passion fruits and mangoes would be great, I think. My little brother is staring at me. He hates me. Are we all going to be able to fit in this car? We can always strap my luggage to the roof.

Dad will drive. No, we'll keep the camera inside the car with me, thank you. The steering wheel is on the wrong side. This is crazy. We're driving on the wrong side of the road and he's aiming for a goat. My plane trip over was wonderful, thank you. That speedometer is wrong. I know we're doing 80. Why do you hate me, little brother? Did you see that gorgeous basket on the woman's head?

This place is the market? You buy food here? I'll come if my luggage is safe. I know Americans are funny. Six shillings are about 50 cents which isn't bad for two papayas, a basket of mangoes and a basket of oranges. Oh, it's really nothing, I just slipped on some rotten mangoes and green things. It won't take long to heal. I'll pass on the sugar-cane for now. Thank you. You actually chew the wood? No, Nairobi is different than Ohio. Oh, you've misunderstood me, I do like it here. I think.

Why are we leaving the city? We're driving into hell. Look at those shacks. Don't the kids have shoes here? Why don't we live in the city? Where exactly is Nairobi

South B? This isn't where we'll live? There aren't phone lines here. Why do you hate me, little brother? This is it? This is home? "Mazungu huko!" Why are all those children screaming "mazungu" at me? Oh, they are only servants yelling "white man." I'm supposed to ignore them. Little brother will chase them away.

This is home now, my new home. This is my new home, a flat in Nairobi South B.

*Dear Mom and Dad, I finally have time to write. Nairobi has beautiful flowers.*

# Wednesday, Oct. 5, 1983

Ms. Odour says "good morning" and everyone is silent and it is expected to be that way. She is big and very black. A Luo, I think, no, I'm sure she is from Kisumu. As on all Tuesdays, and Thursdays, she is wearing her green tie-dye. She looks very African. We say "Good morning Ms. Odour" and the school bell rings.

A pullover isn't warm enough when it's raining out. In the morning there were clouds and the sky is greyish-blue and it looked that way forever. Behind the school is the game reserve, and you could see the blue there until it met the dry grass and the flecks of trees. Maybe giraffes?

I had come late once after lunch, only ten minutes, but it was the "lions'" house meeting day and a prefect was waiting at the gate. I had to run around the school compound in my tie and pullover. The sun was hot and it made my skin itch. People asked what I did to be punished. Everybody was punished for something, but I was white. My face was burning and they teased. It felt good when they laughed. I

wasn't special.

Now a draft comes in from the window and coats the room with a musty and rotting smell. Raindrops hit the windows, pennies into a can, and trickle down with the red dust that settles everywhere. In the front compound, where the morning parades are held, the rain sends red dust into the air.

I drew Opus the penguin on the blackboard once and got caught. Ms. Odour said that I am a bad example. She writes "The Blood Knot" on the board in yellow chalk and we open our books. A single light-bulb is working in the back of the room. Dark and damp. Ms. Odour's face is especially black. Her eyes seemed to bulge.

"'The Blood Knot' is a good play because the white characters are bad." Ms. Odour likes to use me when a white character needs to be read. She repeats words when I don't pronounce them correctly. The Queen's English is better. Schedule with a "sh" sound. Eilliam Ruganda reads the black brother's part and the other students have undecipherable looks on their faces. Ruganda reads with a Kampala accent. Dorcus Thiongo is confused. Ms. Odour is unhappy that I had not really spoken down to the black brother. "I had not acted white," she chastises. "I'll remember to be more condescending," I say. Dorcus doesn't understand "condescending." She is from up-country, Machakos or Nyeri. "How is you?," "What means this?" or "Asanti sana" for everything.

The rain is flooding down and the propped window is closed. The wet air is still coming in from the vent above the door and the single bulb is swaying on its wire. Ms. Odour chooses two new people to continue reading but she looks up from her book to

watch me, my expressions.

"Do American students read African plays?" she wonders.

"African plays? Um, no, I never did," I say.

"Are American schools better?" She leans forward, her eyes wanting to burst. The class is still. Even the rain quiets. "Um." On my paper I dug a line with my thumbnail. The other hand is wet and I smudge the ink. "No," I say. She seems pleased. Dorcus smiles.

Eric Sagwe had asked me before a parade once why America is a super power. People gathered to learn, staring blankly. My shoes and uniform were very new. They noticed. Self-consciously, I had kicked dust on them to hide their shine. Sagwe had rubbed his on the back of his trousers, but the holes stayed. The parade began and the prefects led the school in the singing of the national anthem.

"Ee Mungu nguvu yetu, elete baraka kwetu ..."

The word "prejudice" is being printed on the chalkboard, although much darker than the date or the play title. "Think about it," she says, looking straight at me. "We will talk about it tomorrow."

The bell rings.

**Mark Horak**, North Olmsted, Ohio-Nairobi, Kenya, 1983-84

## Thanks for Sending Our Son to Iowa

I am a mother of an AFS student living now in Audubon, Iowa, at the Jackie Wahlert family since, August 1986. I must write to you some of my (our) feelings and experiences during this time.

Of course, it was very hard for our family when Dirk departed this summer. We miss him urgently and are looking forward to his arrival next summer! But: We also supported him in his plans to spend an AFS year in a foreign country. We wrote to his new family and sent photos, we had several farewell parties and then the day of his departure came.

Well, now four months are gone and this will be the first Christmas without our son. But we'll endure this -- knowing that Dirk has got a wonderful family! All are liking and loving him: the family with the grandparents, his sister-in-law Julie, the neighbors and the kids and his new friends. There were some interviews with big photos in the newspapers (Dirk has sent them all to us), he's making a trip with the school marching-band (Dirk plays saxophone) to Washington DC in June '87 and the family will make holidays after Christmas in Colorado and see the Rocky Mountains!

There is also a close contact to us as we all write regular letters to his host-mother and his sister-in-law. Dirk is writing wonderful long letters with photos and sometimes he calls us. So we know nearly all of his activities and experiences and his new friends.

Especially his birthday I've got to mention: Dirk had his 18th birthday on November 1. As it was Halloween, the AFS chapter invited all foreign students living in their part of Iowa to an AFS-weekend in Audubon. There were 10 girls and boys from Australia, Japan, Brazil, Argentina, Paraguay, Spain, Norway, Denmark, Sweden and Mexico. Dirk told us that they all understood each other very well only after some minutes, as if they were friends all the time. They had a wonderful weekend, and the Halloween/surprise birthday party for our son was a big success and very much fun. In December, there was another AFS weekend in

*Dirk Lehmann and his host mom, Jackie Wahlert.*

Denison, Iowa, and Dirk could meet again his new friends and get to know new families.

You see, we here in Koblenz, Germany, are well-informed and this will show you how happy and proud we are that our son has been chosen by AFS and that he now has the possiblility to make such wonderful experiences!

This is the reason I'm writing to you in your office: We, our family, wants to thank you that you've chosen so well a convenient family for our son. Of course, Iowa isn't just the country we'd wanted or hoped for our son -- you surely know that all students want to come to California or Florida or to the Coast -- but, now we know, that it's more important to have such a warm-hearted family who likes and accepts our son. Therefore, we'll thank you very much.

We wish you a merry Christmas and a blessed New Year.

P.S. Since Dirk's departure, I'm a member of the AFS chapter in Koblenz. I'm also caring for our four AFS students living here: Linda from Pennsylvania, Curtis from Idaho, Gillian from Jamaica and Carola from Paraguay. I'm planning with other members all the activities for them.

Next year, I'm planning to give out our first AFS Newspaper of all the AFS-Chapter-Koblenz with stories, reports and pictures of all the students and host-families; there also will be information about AFS and the programs.

Unfortunately we are a very small chapter. Our members are mostly young AFS students who now are making their graduation and so have less time to help! There are only two men helping me, but we hope that we can find some more people!

My best regards to you all,

**Jutta Lehmann** letter to New York AFS staff (mother of **Dirk**, Koblenz, Germany-Audubon, Iowa 1986-87)

## Too Much Desert

Jay Jasper of Milwaukee, Wisconsin, really wanted to go to an Arabic-speaking country and he was "psyched" to go to Tunisia in North Africa. That he enjoyed himself, learned and grew is undisputed. That he would return at all was in question for a time.

Sometime just before the end of Jay's year in Tunis, 1983-84, he and Austrian AFSer Hannes Langeder decided that they had not really seen the desert. They took a bus as far as they could,

hitched a ride with some truckers and when the last ride ended, they got out and walked. And walked.

They never considered just how far they were going. Sooner than they expected, their water ran out and all around them was desert. Talk about expanding your horizons! All they could see was the horizon. Jay's a pretty cool guy, but he had to be worried. "I mean, it's weird not seeing any living thing except a scorpion," he said.

After three days, they finally saw some people, a group of soldiers who promptly arrested them because it is illegal to wander in the desert and die. Jay thought it was a fine law, indeed.

**M. E.**

*Reminiscent of AFS beginnings--returnees Nelson Graham (Lyndhurst, Ohio-Germany), Johdie Cadorette (Arnold, Maryland-Barbados) and Colleen Armbrust (Menominee, Michigan-Brazil) travelled in a reconditioned ambulance as the AFS Road Show: a singing trio that performed in high schools from Florida to Maine in the spring of 1976.*

# Ulric (Rick) Haynes: From Strength to Strength

AFS enters its 40th year busier than ever, and so does Ulric (Rick) Haynes Jr. The newly installed fifth president of AFS takes the helm of an organization that is transporting more than 8,000 students, journalists and teachers this year to live with families around the globe and which has facilitated the exchanges of nearly 158,000 people from 90 countries over the years.

What more can this former US ambassador to Algeria, businessman and educator accomplish? He articulated his priorities and plans during a March 1987 interview with AFS International Newsletter editor Edie Holbrook.

The new president sees a healthy organization at a crossroad. "AFS has tremendous potential for growth," he said. "We're at a critical juncture in our history in this respect. We have evolved from a US-centered activity to a multinational organization operating programs criss-crossing the world. We are dealing with adult professionals as well as students. And we have charted a major course for ourselves in the developing world. The horizons are limitless."

That will require even greater doses of AFS' vaunted broad-mindedness. "Understanding different notions of voluntarism is critical, especially as we move forward in the developing world," he explained. "The American and European traditions of voluntarism have been the province of those who have a solid socioeconomic base -- who are sufficiently well off to be able to give of themselves. This is not the case in much of the rest of the world.

"However, there are traditions elsewhere which are not labeled 'voluntarism' but which do provide an avenue for achieving the same result. In the Islamic world, for example, the tradition of never turning a stranger away leads to an extraordinary pattern of voluntarism. And the voluntary ethos has its equivalent in the tribal cultures of Africa. These cultural traditions are compatible with the AFS tradition of voluntarism. But they will have to be tapped in ways especially adapted to local culture.

"This entire issue holds implications for our philosophical commitment to socioeconomic diversity. In many parts of the world where we have programs, the reality is that we are dealing with a hosting situation that tends to be elitist. We're dealing in most instances with the middle or wealthy socioeconomic classes."

"The challenge facing AFS," the President continued, "is to give real meaning to our mission by achieving a diverse representation of socioeconomic and ethnic groups in all of our programs. In practical terms, it will necessarily involve developing fresh approaches to recruitment that are uniquely suited to each national environment. It will also involve raising additional funds for scholarships and a constant re-examination of fee-setting."

Within AFS itself, this commitment will mean developing new lines of communication. "A fundamental issue is the need for maximum cooperation in planning. Whatever we do should not be a one-sided perception of what is needed in another part of the world. This involves consultation with and, indeed, taking direction from partner countries, especially in the developing world," he said.

The son of immigrants from Barbados and a proud member of the West Indian-American community, Haynes believes he has an ideal background for his newest challenge. "The opportunity to serve AFS is a wedding of my keen interest in education, international relations and management," he said. " It affords me a unique opportunity to draw upon a wide background of experience to tackle one of our highest priorities, namely the strengthening of the international administration so that AFS can function in a most productive manner."

But Haynes hastens to point out that all work and no play makes AFS a dull organization: "Let me also say that I don't intend to lose sight of what I consider to be a key fringe benefit of operating productively -- having fun and enjoying what we are doing," he said.

## The Role of AFS-- from the 1986 Annual Report

"AFS is an international, nongovernmental, nonprofit organization that promotes intercultural learning through worldwide exchange programs for students, professionals, workers and families

"AFS flies no single flag, represents no single ideology or national objective and speaks no single language. Since its founding by volunteer ambulance drivers of both World Wars, AFS has been a people-to-people movement that transcends national, social, racial, political and religious barriers. It now encompasses 73 countries and links over 100,000 volunteers and 30,000 participants from all regions of the world through ideas, experience and humanitarian ideals.

"Through a wide range of exchange and language programs in which participants live and work or study together, AFS confronts individuals with a world larger than themselves. Participants also gain a more profound cultural understanding of other societies which is essential to the achievement of social justice, peace and harmony in a world of diversity.

"The AFS experience is an apprenticeship for life. On both the personal and professional levels, AFS provides participants with knowledge, communication skills, habits of mind and values that enable them to live and work more effectively in different cultures."

*"Empathy," a sculpture by Dr. Jara Moserova, a 1947 AFSer from Czechoslovakia, presented to AFS in honor of the 25th anniversary of the organization. It is on display in the Galatti Lounge of the AFS International Headquarters, 313 E. 43rd Street in New York City.*

81

## Benefits All-Around

AFS had a profound effect on both my son Paul, who went to Indonesia in 1977, and my daughter Mimi, who went to Finland in 1981, even though they had travelled a lot before.

Our family has discussed how Paul's AFS experience in the Far East opened him up to the life he is now leading in Shanghai. After graduating from college, he went to Taiwan to learn Chinese (while teaching English, to keep "rice on the table"). Now, with his fluent Mandarin, he is the personnel manager at the Shanghai Hilton, currently under construction.

Mimi had very different needs. She lived with a farming family in Finland during the summer of '81 and returned for more than a year in '83 so she could really learn the language. She also taught English for room and board, and although she has come back to the States to finish at the university, she hopes to become a veterinarian and return to a life in Finland.

As their mom, I can say only that AFS is a marvelous program and the Manhattan Beach, Finnish and Indonesian branches of our family all have really benefitted.

**Patricia Woolley,** Manhattan Beach, California

AFS memories, I think it is that one little page in my autograph book that means the most to me. And the first time I read my Australian friend's message, I thought, "Wow, this is really what AFS is all about!"

**Arlene Weintraub,** Arizona-Australia, 1984-85

## What It's All About

During my AFS years in Australia, I encountered a lot of anti-American sentiment. The Australians criticised everything from the Olympics to American foreign policy. And they had no qualms whatsoever about complaining directly to me (as if I had anything to do with it).

I attended an all-girls school in Adelaide, the capital of South Australia. I was the first AFS student to be hosted for the entire year by this school, and the first American most of my classmates had ever met. Many of the girls could not understand why I wasn't pushy, outspoken or violent like many American TV characters. They wanted to know if the streets of the United States were really so dangerous.

I couldn't blame them really; after all, before I went to Australia, I thought I'd see kangaraoos hopping down the streets of the cities! But what was most surprising to my classmates

was how I often agreed with their criticisms of the United States. They were surprised when I told them that I was just as worried as they were that America's defense policies, and our role in the arms race, would someday get the entire world involved in a war.

Anyway, at the end of the school year, everyone passed around autograph books, a ritual

similar to yearbook signing at the end of the year in the US. One girl, who had been particularly open in her criticisms of Americans, wrote a very special message to me. She wrote that I had "changed her mind" about Americans.

In my two large boxes full of

## What Foreigner?

I spent a year trying hard to blend into the physical and cultural ethnicity of my rural Japanese community. Despite my high school uniform (with a hat which had a visor that covered my round eyes), the excitable youngsters in town would spot me, point at me and squeal, "Gaijin!" -- which means foreigner. It was hard to be inconspicuous.

About five months after I arrived, I accompanied three friends through the town. We were walking through a crowd, and as we rounded a corner, my friends suddenly started holding their stomachs in laughter at some private joke.

When I asked what was so funny, they told me that when they heard the word "Gaijin," they reflexively looked around for the foreigner, but this time in vain, for they had forgotten that I, their friend, was the Gaijin!

**Curtis Bartosik,** Greenville, New York-Japan, '82-83

*Right: Goodbye is never easy. Below: An AFS scene familiar to thousands of people: Departure Day madness.*

# Goodbye is Not an Ending

Goodbye is not an ending,
When you know that people care.
For miles may come between us,
But warm thoughts are always there.

Goodbye is not an ending
But a different start for you.
A time for making brand new friends
And seeing dreams come true.

Goodbye is not an ending,
For you'll find along life's way
Within your heart you'll always have
A part of yesterday.

**Bute Kittlesen**, Norway-
Milwaukee, Wisconsin

# INDEX

50th Anniversary Convention, 13
"A World of Difference,"
documentary, 23
A.I.D. (Agency for Int'l
Development), Rhinesmith as
consultant to, 26
Abram, Morris B., 26
Accra, Ghana, 58
Addis Ababa, Ethiopia, 44
Adelaide, South Australia, 82
Africa, 58, 80
AFS Archives, 10
AFS Austria, aid program for
Southeast Asian refugees, 71
AFS Denmark, 20
AFS France, 20
AFS Int'l Council, 26
AFS Int'l Headquarters, 81
AFS Int'l Newsletter, 14, 54, 56,
57, 80
AFS Ireland, 70
AFS Italy, 32
AFS Koblenz, 78
AFS Peru, 71
AFS Program Support, 57
AFS Road Show, 79
AFS Switzerland, 71
AFS Thailand, 40
AFS World, 63
AFS World Review, 32
AFS, internationalization of, 27
AFS-EURAFME (Europe, Africa
and the Middle East), 59
AFS-LACAP (Latin America,
Canada, and the Pacific), 58, 59
AFS-USA Board, 20
AFSC (American Friends Service
Committee), 26
AFSIS, 1
Akron, Ohio, 45
Algeria, Haynes as US
Ambassador to, 80
Amazonas, Brazil, 60
American Magazine, The, 4
Andrew, A. Piatt "Doc," 1
Applewhite, Robert "Apple," 5,
13
Aransas Wildlife Refuge, 73
Argentina, 9, 46, 78
Arizona, 82
Armbrust, Colleen, 79
Arnold, Maryland, 79

Artigas, Uruguay, 75
Auckland, New Zealand, 70
Audubon, Iowa, 78
Australia, 10, 28, 33, 39, 43, 72,
73, 78
Austria, 28, 79
Austwell, Texas, 73
Bailey, Judy, 20
Baker, Edith, 70
Bangkok, Thailand, 40
Barbados, 79, 80
Barcelona, Spain, 8
Barcia, Reynaldo, 16
Bartosik, Curtis, 82
Bartschi, Joyce, 12
Bashford, Robyn, 43
Belfast, Northern Ireland, 22, 23
Belize, Central America, 40
Bella Union, Uruguay, 73, 74
Bernhardt, Martha, 73
Bernstein, Leonard, 26
Big Sky Resort, Montana, 20
Billings, Montana, 20
Blue Mountains, 41
Bohorquez, Lilly, 75
Bombay, India, 32
Borneo (Indonesia), 9
Boston University, 46
Brazil, 73, 78, 79
Brehm, Carolyn, 32
Brewster, Kingman Jr., 26
Brooke, Edward W., 26
Brookfield, Connecticut, 46
Brown, Dr. Bill, 6
Burdick, Sally Hermans, 30
Burgoyne, Odile, 18
Bus trip, 4, 5, 43
Butler, Wisconsin, 75
Byrne, Carol, 55
C.W. Post Orientation, 28, 40,
62, 63, 69
Cadaces, Costa Brava, Spain, 8
Cadorette, Johdie, 79
California, 13, 72, 78,
Camp Hill, Pennsylvania, 46
Canyon de Chelly, 72
Carcianiga, Chiara, 60
Ceylon (now Sri Lanka), 34, 59
Chile, 58
Chinese Teachers Program, 70
Chinle, Arizona, 72
Claremore, Oklahoma, 50
Clayton, Lorna, 70
Cleveland, Ohio, 70
Clinton, Iowa, 37

Cody, Wyoming, 20
Colombia, 47
Colombo, Sri Lanka, 34
Colorado, 78
Columbia University, 4
Colvin, Jean, 44
Connecticut, 59
Cook's Bay, New Zealand, 50
Copenhagen, Denmark, 30
Coppage, Jacquie, 49
Corona, California, 30
Correa, Juan Carlos, 25, 58
Cosart, Nanette, 72
Costa Rica, 31, 39
Craig, Jackie, 57
Crawford, Sir Frederick, 11
Crawford, US Ambassador
William R., 25
Cronkite, Walter, 2
Cross, Kirsten, 72
Cyprus Broadcasting
Corporation, 24
Cyprus, 24-25, 58
Czechoslovakia, 18, 81
Dallas, Patrick, 72
Dar es Salaam, Tanzania, 11
de Gregori, James, 73-75, Gayle,
73, Roger, 73-5
Denison, Iowa, 78
Denmark, 18, 62, 78
Des Moines, Iowa, 4, 55
Devereux, Mark, 72
Director-General, title retired, 13
Dixon, Lisa, 28
Dobbs Ferry, New York, 7
Domestic Program, 21, in Italy,
Switzerland and the US, 26
Douglas, Arizona, 72
Dublin, Ireland, 70
Dubuque, Iowa, 44
Dundee, New South Wales,
Australia, 70
Dusseldorf, Germany, 18
Dyal, Bill, 52-54, 59
Eagle Letters, 1, 15, 17
Eastern Illinois University
Midyear Conference, 61
Ecuador, 16
Ede, the Netherlands, 30
Edgell, George, 1, 13, 15
Edinburgh, Scotland, 21
Egypt, 58, 63
Eisenhower, Dwight D., 4
El Salvador, 47
El-Said, Howaida, 63